Spellcrafting

The Ultimate Spellcraft Guide for Beginners Wanting to Create Spells and Learn Spellcasting

Your Free Gift
(only available for a limited time)

Thanks for getting this book! If you want to learn more about various spirituality topics, then join Mari Silva's community and get a free guided meditation MP3 for awakening your third eye. This guided meditation mp3 is designed to open and strengthen ones third eye so you can experience a higher state of consciousness. Simply visit the link below the image to get started.

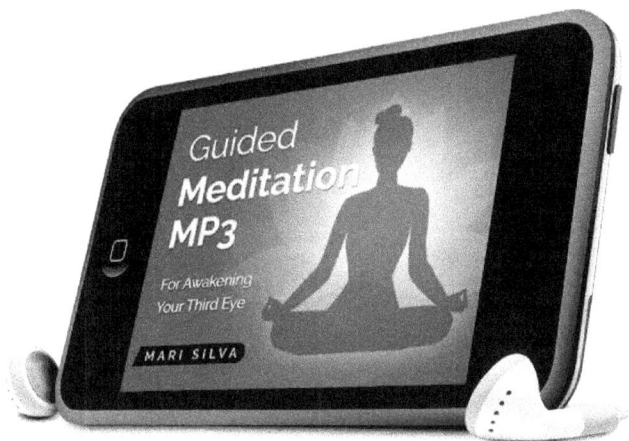

https://spiritualityspot.com/meditation

Table of Contents

Introduction

Are you interested in increasing your knowledge about spellcrafting even further? As an ancient art that contributed a lot to several religions and cultures worldwide, spellcrafting is a great skill to master. It is the key to creating spells and magic that will work to your best advantage.

If you like anything related to spells and magic, this book about spellcrafting can help. With this reading material, you will have a practical, easy-to-follow, and accessible guide containing all the things you should know about crafting and casting effective spells. This means that spells, otherwise called witches' prayers, are those that everyone can learn and eventually master.

The good news is that you don't have to get involved in a mystery cult or promise to serve a god or goddess so you can start crafting spells. You don't also need to convert to or denounce a religion. All you have to do is read this book and grasp every bit of information included here.

The details included in this reading material are all easy to understand and follow. Even those concepts that are otherwise difficult to understand are simplified to ensure that readers will not have a hard time absorbing their meanings and significance. Most of the instructions about casting spells included here are also practical and easy to apply.

After reading this book, you will surely have a much clearer understanding of spells and magic. You will know how magical energy works and the secrets to spellcrafting. With that, you will be on your way towards tapping your inner power and focus, so you can guide and direct them while you use just simple items and ingredients.

Just make sure you also have an open mind, patience, will, courage, self-conviction, and genuine desire before following what's instructed in this book. With all the mentioned qualities, you can easily follow what is in your heart and be mature enough to take full responsibility for every step and action you undertake as you start crafting your own spells.

Chapter 1 – The Art of Spellcrafting

First and foremost, spellcrafting, also called spell-making, is an art in the world of magic. It is the art of crafting or creating unique spells either by making your own from scratch or by combining different spells that are already existing. If you use existing spells, you can modify or change them a bit so you can use them for your desired result.

Remember that trying to learn the art of spellcrafting requires a lot of patience, as it takes time for you to master it and put your knowledge to practical use. Customizing your spells is likely to produce more than one effect, like fire and frost damage.

The effect's magnitude will also be proportional to the specific magic needed in casting the spell. Several effects also tend to meet compounding magic requirements.

Spell Defined

In its basic form, a spell refers to your intent to enforce a change using energy. You can manifest it in various ways. It could be through dancing and chanting or elaborate rituals that require the participation of many people for a few days,

There are instances when rituals are only spiritual, practiced mainly to honor a deity or celebrate an important holiday. The rituals, therefore, do not necessarily require the presence of spells. Also, note that sometimes, spells have physical ingredients. At the same time, in other instances, they need nothing else except for the energy you are raising. However, every spell has similar basic components regardless of how elaborate it is.

One more fact about spells is that even if they are common, you can't perceive them immediately as inherently religious. They do not also necessarily form part of just a single practice. As a matter of fact, contrary to what a lot of people believe, the majority of religions worldwide use spells – among which are Christians. Take the act of prayer as an example.

Every time you pray, you tend to set an intent, raise your energy, then release it to the universe. The process may also involve summoning a sort of deity so you can receive aid in manifesting your prayer. In most cases, you can expect the deity to perform almost all the legwork for you, which lessens the activity on your part. With that, it is no longer surprising to see prayer being easily distinguishable compared to other active types and forms of spellwork.

The act of crafting and casting spells is not also just contemporary; spells have existed since prehistoric times, making it a truly ancient magical practice. Aside from that, remember that while you can look at prayer as a religious act, the use of spells is usually secular.

This means that anyone can access spells regardless of what religion they believe in. With that, it is no longer surprising to find witches who practice the art of spellcrafting and witchcraft while strongly believing in Jesus and God.

The Art of Spellcrafting and Witchcraft for Beginners

As mentioned just a while ago, spellcrafting is an art that requires a lot of time, patience, and commitment to master. Contrary to what many believe, learning witchcraft, magic, and the art of crafting spells is not easy. It is not a quick way to gain your desired results and rewards. It is more than just following instructions, like lighting a candle and saying some words; there is so much more involved in the process.

For instance, you can view spells as art resembling recipes. The reason is that they allow you to follow along. However, suppose you are unfamiliar with the ingredients and the techniques. In that case, the entire process will likely be a hit or miss. As you depend more on the recipe without comprehending the things that compose them and what makes them work, it is also highly probable that you will experience more misses instead of hits.

The same premise is applicable in witchcraft and spellcrafting. Like any other skill, it involves more than just following recipe instructions. You have to understand every component and element of it to judge if it is good enough or has flaws. In other words, the whole process is more than just sticking to spells written by other people.

Merely trusting it is not enough. It is not also enough to adhere to and follow the instructions and hope that the best outcome comes from it. It requires learning everything about the spell. You have to be familiar with the components (ingredients) and the techniques and tools used in the process.

Spellcrafting and spellcasting are, therefore, not as easy as writing some words and expressing them aloud as you wave a wand or piece of wood while anticipating that it will produce your desired results. It involves a lot of work, including the gathering of information and spell ingredients. Some deep reflection is also necessary. You should think of what you do and why.

For instance, you need to think of and reflect on what you ask or expect a certain gemstone or herb to do for you. By doing that, you will be able to make your mind focus or concentrate. Also, you have to ensure that every word in your spell is concise and well thought out. This should not leave any room for misinterpretation or confusion.

The Language of Magic

When it comes to spellcrafting, make it a point to truly understand the language of magic. Note that words are not only elements of writing or speech, as they are also powerful enough that you can use them to strengthen the effects of a spell or magic. Speaking the words aloud can even transform them into vibrations and frequencies.

You can use the right vibrations and frequencies to control and direct energy. Since the vibrations and frequencies of words hold power designed to keep energy under control, learning and understanding how you can use the correct magic words should be the first thing you should do in spellcrafting and creating magic effects.

Also, remember that the words you will use in magic can be expressed in various forms. You can say them in the form of not only spells but also prayers, incantations, and songs. The reason why they are in various forms is that words have a great impact on the world we are presently living in.

Words spoken with a sound are also useful in directing energy – the kind of energy that can produce magical effects. Once you know how to do that, you will realize that words hold the same power as swords.

Traditional Words Used in Magic and Spells

As you may have already known by now, words play a major role in the world of making and crafting spells. The language you use in your spells can have a say on how effective they will be. Some of the most commonly used traditional and empowered words in the world of magic are the following:

Abracadabra

This seemingly nonsense word that has already been passed on several generations is very impressive. Originally, the word *abracadabra* was already considered magic. Ever since, many magicians, witches, spell makers, and casters have used the word *abracadabra* as a form of charm that gives them protection against every kind of evil, as well as illness and bad luck.

At that time, the word was supposedly written on one piece of papyrus several times. The last letter of the word has to be dropped on every line until the one who practiced magic successfully reduced the word into just one letter, specifically the letter "a," which is the last one.

Once the word abracadabra reached the English during the 16th century, many no longer used it as a physical charm. It turned into an incantation designed to offer protection from evil. After several centuries, the abracadabra word started to lose a lot of its mystical potency. Upon reaching the 19th century, abracadabra turned into a word you can connect with conjurers.

Hocus Pocus

There is also the word *hocus pocus*, which you can associate with the process of executing some transformation or trick. This word also underwent a bit of tricky and challenging transformation.

When the word "hocus pocus" came to English during the early 1600s, it was specifically used to describe jugglers. When the 1600 century was coming to an end, the word hocus-pocus started to be used to refer to the cry of a conjurer, the sleight of hand, or as a reference to a form of nonsense or trickery.

Open Sesame

Who has not heard of the word "open sesame"? A famous line in the movies, open sesame is also ideal for use in the world of magic and spellcrafting. Before the 1600s, this line became a famous opening spell that provided wizards passage even in locked doors. This happens by ripping the doors from the hinges and then letting them get torn to the firewood. You can also use this powerful word in modern spells, especially if you intend to open up something positive, like certain opportunities.

Modern-day Spellcrafting

When it comes to modern-day spellcrafting, strengthening your mind is a necessity. The reason is that the most vital tool when it comes to creating spells is no longer the candle, the cauldron, or the spell book; it is your mind. Developing a stronger mind means you will also improve at creating spells. You need a strong mental aptitude in modern-day spellcrafting so you can do the following:

- Retain your focus for a prolonged period
- Move willingly from one phase of consciousness to another
- Improve your sensory abilities and perceptions
- Gain access to the untapped components of your subconscious and conscious minds with ease
- Manipulate or control your energy – You raise, hold, release, or direct it.

Strengthening your mind works similarly to when you are strengthening your other muscles. You can also do a few psychic exercises designed to boost your mental abilities. Aside from that, you can try meditation, as it is a great way to train your mind to become even stronger.

A lot of traditional tools for Wicca have a strong association with witchcraft. Several of these tools were the ones inherited from ceremonial magic. The good thing about them is that they tend to work well. It is the reason why people, regardless of their paths, make use of them.

Modern witchcraft and spellcrafting, therefore, give practitioners, often the average people, the freedom to work on anything based on their own preferences rather than using traditional tools. As an important tip, you must learn and understand the tools you intend to use. Try experimenting with them and determining the specific ones that suit your personality and needs the most.

In modern spellcrafting, there is no need to get a cauldron or any other traditional tool if you feel like it is unnecessary. Some find it an indispensable part of the process of creating and casting spells. Still, if you feel you don't need one, you can use other tools that fit your preference and personal style.

Also, contrary to what the media depicts, witchcraft can be just a basic art. It is not exclusively meant for evil purposes, unlike what the media in the form of movies and other forms of entertainment demonstrate. As a matter of fact, you can use spells to attract everything that is good and positive or to ward off evil and negative energy from your home and life.

If your mind is extremely well-disciplined, you can practice this magic form without any tools. Still, most modern practitioners feel like they should use some tools designed to improve their focus and symbolize whatever it is they want from the spells. They also use these tools in drawing, borrowing, and manipulating energies.

In the beginning, there is a high chance that you will greatly depend on certain tools when crafting and making spells. Once you master everything, you can drop such reliance on the tools, especially once you notice your mind becoming stronger. You can start relying on the power of your mind to make spells that work.

The Wiccan Rede

When it comes to the ethical practice of crafting and casting spells, the Wiccan Rede tends to play a very vital role. Before you complete any spell or ritual, you need to fully understand the Wiccan Rede, which only consists of eight powerful words that remind practitioners to never do any harm.

"An Ye Harm None, Do What Ye Will"

The Wiccan rede has a full version, which is longer, but it revolves around that 8-word code of conduct. By taking to heart what the Wiccan rede states, you will be fully guided in practicing the art of spellcrafting. You will know exactly how you should act and perform magickal work while ensuring that you also take responsibility for every action you take. It serves as your way to practice magick ethically.

The same guideline or rule is what you can find in Aleister Crowley's works wherein he offered advice to his readers through this line, *"Do what thou wilt shall be the whole of the law. Love is the law, love under will"*.

Crowley coined the term "magick," which means that it is an actual term, not a typo or a misspelling. Magick was mostly used by Thelemic and ceremonial practitioners. Crowley coined this term to differentiate and show the occult associated with performing magic.

Magick practitioners also define it as a science and art aiming to stimulate change while confirming with the will. It even encompasses mundane acts of will and ritual magic.

Crowley also perceived magick as a vital technique for anyone who intends to gain a real understanding of themselves and act based on their true will. It, therefore, serves as a way to reconcile free will and destiny. In his writings, he explained that, theoretically, it is possible to trigger a change in any object that is naturally capable of doing that.

As far as the Wiccan Rede, and all its other versions, including that of Crowley, are concerned, they mainly serve as a simple guideline. Note that you can't find universal ethical standards and rules for modern pagans and magic practitioners. With that, it is unreasonable to assume that all pagans will adhere to the Wiccan Rede.

Still, it would be much better for you to stick to the Wiccan rede of not doing any harm whenever you craft and cast spells. If you want to practice spellcrafting, you have to constantly remind yourself of your good intention.

Combined with your thoughtful action, your intention will come to life while ensuring that you practice the art of making and casting spells based on ethics. This means that even if you are performing a sort of magic, you still treat everyone with respect and fairness.

By performing magic and creating spells based on ethics and what is right, you will surely be able to make the most out of it, allowing yourself to bask in the power of being one with the energies and rhythms of the earth.

Chapter 2 – Elements and Magickal Correspondences

Correspondences are among the most vital parts of crafting and casting spells. You have to consider these correspondences every time you practice the art of spellcrafting. Note that colors, scents, and symbols are primary components of all forms of spells as they are capable of stimulating your senses while setting your overall tone.

In the world of magic, correspondences serve as representations of the relationship between natural and magical realities or between physical and psychic realities. It is not a new concept and idea, really, but the first time relational terminology was established was during the 18th century. It was coined by Emanuel Swedenborg, a theologian during that time, in his works, including Heaven and Hella and the Arcana Coelestia.

Swedenborg's proposal legitimized the notions and philosophies of correspondences that were already long-held between things, like speech and thought, action and intention, body and mind, and physical and psychic planes. The correspondences recognized between one's physical and psychic planes of operation and existence extend to every object found in the physical world.

For instance, you can expect the light to have a strong correspondence to wisdom, considering that wisdom can enlighten your mind. In contrast, light works to enlighten the eye. The same principle can be applied to warmth. Warmth strongly corresponds to love since love can warm the mind in such a way that heat warms the body.

With the proven importance of magical correspondences, it is no longer surprising to see a table listing all concepts, objects, and beings perceived to have a strong connection to supernatural beings. You can find these correspondence tables in many modern books that talk about the occult and magic. You can use them as reference tools in crafting and casting them. We will tackle some of the correspondences that you can find in such tables here.

Elemental Correspondences

The elemental correspondences encompass fire, water, air, and earth. They serve as the classical elements of magic that also have the fifth in the form of spirit, quintessence, or aether, which serves as the binding force. One important fact about these elements/elemental correspondences is that they embody the realms of the cosmos, which is where you can expect things to exist.

The classic thinking of the Greeks made them categorize the elemental correspondences based on water content and temperature. For instance, the air is mainly moist and secondarily warm. Then there is fire, which is mainly warm and secondarily dry; water, which is mainly cool, then secondarily moist; and earth, which is mainly dry and cool secondarily.

Modern-day paganism also puts a lot of focus and emphasis on the mentioned four elements. Each element has a strong connection to meanings and traits and the compass directions.

Also, note that in the world of magick, the different elements here serve as determinants. You can see these elements represented on the pentagram, with each one having various properties playing vital roles in the workings and preparations of rituals.

The elements symbolize the states, polarities, elevation levels, and directions, among many others. These elemental correspondences are also vital as they comprise two polarities – one of which is active while the other is passive. Remember that the universe has no such thing as bad or good. The reason is that specific laws and principles govern everything.

Moreover, in terms of preparing rituals, the Supreme power will be the one who will choose the specific number of elements you can use. That said, expect some rituals to need just one element while others need at least two elements.

To give you an even better idea about the elemental correspondences, here are the elements and their representations.

Earth

The earth element strongly represents stability, wisdom, security, strength, permanence, abundance, wealth, materialism, patience, responsibility, truth, prosperity, and practicality. Some of the symbols used when referring to the earth are rocks, mountains, soil, trees, and the earth itself. The earth is also recognized as the most dependable and stable of all the elements. It can sustain life and is known for being so stable that other elements also rely on it.

- **Direction** - North
- **Color** - Green
- **Qualities** - heavy and passive, cold and dry
- **Metal** - Mercury, lead
- **Zodiac signs** - Virgo, Capricorn, Taurus
- **Types of magic** - Tree magic, fertility magic, rune casting, prosperity, herbal lore, knot magic
- **Season** - Winter
- **Celtic name** - Tuath
- **Hour of the day** - Midnight
- **Alchemical symbol** - upside-down triangle while having a line in the middle
- **Symbols** - Caves, fields, gems, rocks, mountains
- **Symbolic creatures** - Stag, bull, sphinx
- **Plants** - Thrift plant, red poppy, grains, ivy

Air

Air strongly connects to the mind, intelligence, and mental process. This element is creative and works in such a way that it can lead to the manifestation of your magical intentions. You can also see it as having a strong connection with wisdom, higher consciousness, purification, and divination.

It also symbolizes inspiration, communication, clarity, freedom, ideas, dreams and wishes, and the capacity to know and understand, among many others. Some rituals related to air require you to toss a few objects in the wind, play a wind instrument or flute, hang certain objects in high places or trees, and burn aromatherapy and incense.

- **Direction** - East
- **Color** - Yellow
- **Qualities** - light and active, hot and moist
- **Metal** - Mercury, aluminum, tin
- **Zodiac signs** - Libra, Gemini, Aquarius
- **Types of magic** - Finding a lost or stolen object, divination, visualization, magic of four winds
- **Season** - Spring
- **Celtic name** - Airt
- **Hour of the day** - Dawn
- **Alchemical symbol** - right side up triangle while having a line in the middle
- **Symbols** - Wind, sky, incense, clouds
- **Symbolic creatures** - Hawk, eagle, butterfly
- **Plants** - Mistletoe, aspen tree

Fire

The fire element is also important in the world of magic as it is a symbol of change, inspiration, energy, life force, passion, sexuality, love, faith, trust, leadership, spirit, innocence, elusiveness, and will. It symbolizes self-healing, renewal, personal and physical vulnerability, protection, and relationship with yourself and others.

The fire element also has a link to passion and change. It is spiritual and physical, as it is linked to both divinity and sexuality. You can also expect fire magic to quickly fill and manifest with primal energy.

- **Direction** – South
- **Color** – Red
- **Qualities** – light and active, hot and dry
- **Metal** – Gold, brass, steel, iron
- **Zodiac signs** – Aries, Sagittarius, Leo
- **Types of magic** – Healing, tantra, candle magic
- **Season** – Summer
- **Celtic name** – Deas
- **Hour of the day** – Noon
- **Alchemical symbol** – right side up triangle
- **Symbols** – Fire, volcanoes, stars, sun, hearth fire, candle flame
- **Symbolic creatures** – fire-breathing dragons, lions, horses
- **Plants** – Red poppies, onions, garlic, nettle

Water

The water element represents feelings, absorption, purification, intuition, unconscious/subconscious mind, courage, emotions, wisdom, self-healing, psychic ability, reflection, vision quests, and eternal movement. It also encompasses every emotional aspect of femininity and love.

The water element strongly relates to your intuition, emotions, and subconscious mind. Since it is a primal component of life, the womb symbolizes this element and makes it relevant to fertility. As for the rituals you can do with the aid of the water element, some examples are ritual bathing, tossing some objects into water, sprinkling, washing, diluting, and brewing.

- **Direction** – West
- **Color** – Blue
- **Qualities** – Heavy and passive, cold and moist
- **Metal** – Silver, copper
- **Zodiac signs** – Scorpio, Cancer, Pisces

- **Types of magic** - Mirror magic, healing, purification, fertility, dream magic, divination
- **Season** - Fall
- **Celtic name** - Iar
- **Hour of the day** - Twilight
- **Alchemical symbol** - Upside down triangle
- **Symbols** - Bodies of water, rain, waterfalls, fog, waves
- **Symbolic creatures** - All water creatures, snakes, scorpions, dragons or serpents, dolphin
- **Plants** - All water plants, lotus, fern, moss

Spirit

Lastly, there is what we call the spirit element. It is almost identical to the fire element. Note that there are times when spiritual entities, like nature spirits, ancestors, and Gods, become recognized as spiritual elements in ritual. It also represents most things considered spiritual, including goddesses, omnipresence, immanence, transcendence, and the center of the universe.

- **Direction** - Center
- **Color** - White, purple, black, rainbow
- **Qualities** - Being spaceless, timelessness
- **Metal** - Meteorite
- **Season** - Cycle itself
- **Time** - Beyond time, solar and lunar cycles
- **Symbols** - Spiral, the cosmos
- **Symbolic creatures** - Sphinx, owl

The Moon Phases and Their Importance

Aside from the mentioned elemental correspondences, you should know that moon phases and sun energy will play a crucial role in spellcrafting and making magic. All witches and witchcraft practitioners fully know how powerful moon phases are. They have used these moon phases ever since to give them courage, guidance, success, and luck in crafting and casting spells.

They also use the power of the moon phases to heighten the power of their spellwork. The fact that the moon is a heavenly body, which is the closest to the sky, also means that it can greatly influence your life and the results of your spellwork. If you want to practice witchcraft, you can use the moon phases when timing your magic. Doing so can increase the power of your spells.

Here are the primary moon phases to guide you in timing your magic. Each of these moon phases has its own special energies and power.

New Moon (Phase 1)

Considered the first phase, the new moon serves as a representation of a fresh start. The moon in the first phase is hardly visible as the sky may look black. There are instances when magic is quite literal, so while the moon is in the phase wherein it is not visible, it is the perfect time to perform shadow work. You can also use this phase to recognize your dark sides or hide or shadow yourself.

For example, you are aware that you are somewhat manipulative. Still, whenever someone calls you out about it, you feel the need to defend yourself or deny the presence of such a trait. In this case, you can use the new moon to explore your shadow side (for example. your manipulative side) and look for ways you can positively work with it.

It is the perfect time to look for healthy ways to use such skills, like building a much better career without the risk of hurting others. You may also want to use your manipulative side to read others to convince your partner of the importance of communicating together instead of being the only one in control.

The fact that the new moon represents new beginnings also means that it is the perfect moment to set your intentions and goals for the next cycle. This first phase should encourage beginnings, like falling in love. To set yourself off to a new beginning, you need to release yourself from the past.

Let go of everything that happened in the past, especially negative ones. The new moon will always have your back anytime you wish to clear the path of your love life and remove all the bad energies in it. This is a good thing in your attempt to find your ideal mate.

- **Rising and setting time** - Dawn and sunset
- **Time** - From the first time the new moon appears and three and a half days after
- **Pagan Holiday** - Winter solstice
- **Purpose** - Beginnings
- **Offering** - Milk and honey
- **Theme** - Abundance
- **Magic** - Divination, health, deconstructive magic and curses, business, love, self-improvement, beauty

Waxing Moon (Phase 2)

In this phase, expect the moon to become luminous literally. It will look like a fascinating orb appearing in the sky. The waxing moon phase serves as the time for you to prioritize the specific areas of your life that you have longed to focus on, like personal aspects, including empathy, self-discovery, and love. Reflect on the things that make you completely happy.

Focus on crafting spells for your personal betterment and improving your sense of happiness and fulfillment. Also, note that during this phase, the waxing moon tends to grow and become even brighter. It, therefore, creates a perfect phase for you to perform sympathetic magic surrounding growth.

The energy the waxing moon provides can also support you when it comes to attracting, drawing, constructing, and manifesting things to yourself. That said, you can use these energies in crafting spells for improvement, like in areas of spiritual growth, career, finance, love, job opportunities, creativity, and positivity.

- **Rising and setting time** - Mid-morning and sunset
- **Time** - Three and a half to seven days after the new moon came out
- **Pagan Holiday** - Imbolc
- **Purpose** - Movement of things
- **Offering** - Candles
- **Theme** - Manifestation

- **Magic** – Animal magic, attraction spells, friendships, inner beauty, protection, success, luck, wealth, healing, psychic work, change, emotions

Full Moon (Phase 3)

Many consider this third phase, the full moon, as the strongest out of all the moon phases. In astrology, the full moon comes out when the moon and the sun are on opposing sides. During this phase, expect a lot of emotions to run high, making everything all the more intense.

The good news is that you can take advantage of this intensity by making it a part of your spells while knowing that there is a bright ball of power that continues to shine upon you and help you. Some practitioners even make it a point to charge their crystals during this phase. They just put their crystals in a spot that gets them exposed to the light shone by the full moon.

You can also create full-moon water. All you have to do is put a glass of water in a place where the full moon's light shines on it. Make it a point to put the glass or goblet containing the water above your letter of intention. Leave the water there so the full moon can charge it. You may then use the full moon water as part of your spells and rituals.

Also, note that the intensity of the full moon may cause you to feel extremely heavy in case there are certain emotional issues that you are currently avoiding or processing. That said, honor what your body is telling you during this time. If you feel it is asking for more rest and sleep, give it that.

- **Rising and setting time** – Sunset and dawn
- **Time** – Fourteen to seventeen days and a half after the new moon appeared
- **Pagan Holiday** – Summer solstice
- **Purpose** – Project completion
- **Offering** – Flowers
- **Theme** – Power
- **Magic** – Health, beauty, divination, healing, fitness, psychic work, romance, banishing, love, dreams, change, protection,

motivation, family, money, psychic work, clarity

Waning Moon (Phase 4)

The waning moon refers to the period when the moon becomes darker again. It moves from the full moon and then back to the new moon. In this fourth phase, you can perform banishing work. For instance, you could cut cords with a lover in the past. Note, though, that banishing a specific person completely from your life is not the only thing you can do under this phase.

You can also perform other powerful banishing spells, like those that eliminate your toxic or bad feelings for someone. You can also work on banishing your self-doubts and insecurities when the waning moon phase comes. It is an incredible moment to empower yourself instead of changing another's will.

You can use it to eliminate anything that you consider negative, toxic, or bad for you, including unfair treatment in the workplace or your imposter syndrome. Get rid of unwanted negativities, particularly those that tend to keep you from enjoying and living your life to the fullest.

Reflect on things that block you from reaching your goals. Pay attention to energy and roadblocks so you can release yourself from anything hindering you from attaining your desired goals.

- **Rising and setting time** – Mid-evening and Mid-morning
- **Time** – Three and a half to seven days after the full moon appeared
- **Pagan Holiday** – Lammas
- **Purpose** – Initial destruction
- **Offering** – Rice or grain
- **Theme** – Reassessment
- **Magic** – Addictions, emotions, banishing, cleansing, divorce, protection, undoing curses and bindings

Dark Moon (Phase 5)

Lastly, there is the dark moon, a particularly powerful moon phase that occurs before the next lunar cycle. All spells during this special moon phase have to be well-thought-out. This phase is a time to work on something bigger than you – one that is beyond what is personal. It should let you deal with bigger situations and concerns involving more than one person, like in the case of divorce, death, or addiction.

For instance, if you have bad habits, like smoking, that you want to get rid of, then the dark moon phase is the best time for you to do it. You can create a spell designed to strengthen your willpower so you will succeed in quitting your unwanted habits.

It is also in the dark moon wherein you can reflect deeply on your passion and anger while asking for strength and compassion. You can perform dark moon spells in 10 and ½ to 14 days after the full moon's arrival.

Some witches avoid casting spells during the dark moon. However, others consider it as the best time for workings. In terms of magic, the dark moon is designed for divination. Aside from banishing unhelpful and unwanted habits, you can also banish spells during this phase to eliminate energies and relationships.

A lot of witches also take advantage of the dark moon phase to do spells linked to completely removing something from their life. Some also use it to cleanse so they will come fully prepared for the new moon.

The Sun Energy and Its Importance in Spellcrafting

In a lot of Pagan traditions at present, you will likely notice them putting more emphasis on the power, energies, and magic of the moon. It is not the only heavenly body you can take advantage of regarding spellcrafting and witchcraft.

While sometimes ignored and taken for granted, the sun is extremely important in spells, especially if you consider it a source of magic, myth, and legend for several decades.

Similar to the moon, the sun also has its own cycles. Basically, there are two cycles for the sun, namely, the day and the year. Also called the wheel of the year, the yearly cycle works by increasing the sun's power until Litha (when it reaches its peak power). After that, the sun's power leaks off as the wheel approaches the spectrum of darkness.

Some find the daily sun cycle more convenient. In this cycle, you will notice the sun's power increasing until noontime when it reaches the peak point in the sky. Upon falling towards the horizon, expect the power of the sun to wane. As for the sunset, many consider it a liminal time. It signifies that the sunset is visible in between two worlds.

Summer Sun Energies

When the summer months come, the sun's energy will become most efficient for specific classifications and categories of working. It is like when the waxing moon comes with different intentions from those of the waning moon. Sure, you can do all sorts of magic any time you wish, but remember that your spellwork will be more efficient when you perfect your timing.

Generally, the summer creates sure and strong energy; logically, it follows that performing magic about health, healing, and beauty will be more effective during this time. It also assists greatly in spells promoting love and other relationships.

If you wish to restart a project, you can use the summer sun as your ultimate energy source. One important fact to remember is that the summer sun energies tend to change as time passes. With that, expect them to be divided based on sun signs, namely Leo, Virgo, and Cancer.

Cancer

Starting from the 22nd of June to the 23rd of July, there's a chance for Cancer energies to be at their strongest or peak. "Home and Hearth" are the themes for this time of year. In other words, your family, your closest relationships, and your abode. This is the optimum time for spellwork regarding your emotions.

Leo

The Lion (July to August 22) encompasses strength and courage, creativity and showmanship, willpower, and fertility. Use his energies wisely and copiously for success.

Strongly linked to physical appearances, Leo is particularly helpful when trying for a healthy and beautiful glow - and for weight loss. Last – but not least – use Leo's energies to work on pride (the good kind), generosity of heart, and ambitiousness (again, the good kind!)

Virgo

Virgo is the last component of summer, from around the 23rd of August to the 22nd of September. The energy and vibe of this sign demonstrate self-improvement, organization, and service. You can also make Virgo energies work for you if there is a certain problem you have to analyze.

For instance, if your goal is to contribute to solving global issues, such as poverty or hunger, then you should consider doing it during this specific period. Virgo also contributes to dealing with certain issues that revolve around your health, mental energies, ability to pay attention to detail, responsibilities, and employment.

Daily Sun Cycle

If you want to take advantage of the sun's daily cycle, learning about the following phases composing the cycle can help.

Sunrise

Most feel at their freshest and highest level of energy upon waking up in the morning. With that, it is the best time to do magical work. Note that the morning sun will always serve as an incredible source of energy. You may want to begin your day with a ritual, which contributes to making you feel at your best even more.

Cast your charms in the morning's sun to rid yourself of the negative energies floating around you. This is also the time best time to fight addictions.

With its ability to start your day, the morning sun works best for any form of magic concerning those you can begin in the morning, such as school or business.

Midday

The midday involves the sun energies after lunchtime. It is considered the highest point or peak in the sky, considering that the sun's energy level is at its highest at this time of the day. With the great strength of the sun during midday, you can use it to overcome all weaknesses you intend to get rid of. You can cast your spell at lunchtime under the bright and high sun in case you want to be inspired or guided.

Sunset

As for the sunset, it is certainly a special time of the day. It is when the colors you can see above the sky promote the cooling of the ground. The ground also tends to cool down as the sunset comes with darkness and a soft breeze. The dusk will always be the perfect moment for relaxation. It will boost your willpower, serenity, and calmness.

Also considered "a liminal time," sunset is a time between worlds, allowing for unbelievable magic to take place! Between day and night, this liminal time is perfect for adjusting to changes.

Chapter 3 – The Spellcrafter's Toolkit

As a beginner in crafting and casting spells – and the world of magic and witchcraft in general – among the first few things that you may be wondering about is the specific tools you need to create your own spells and cast them. There are several tools that a spellcrafter can use. Note, though, that all the recommended special tools are not one hundred percent necessary.

The reason is that, in reality, it would be unnecessary to use any special tools since the magic relies on the actual practitioner. Also, witchcraft and spellcrafting revolve around meanings. This means that the tools you should use have a specific meaning and identity that you can uniquely link to. The connection is what will provide you with the power you need for the practice.

You have to know the importance of every ingredient and tool used in crafting and casting spells. By doing that, you can successfully form magic rituals and spells that you can use in building a path designed to make your life more meaningful and spiritual.

Over time, the tools you decide to use for all your spells will be a major part of you. They will help define your identity as a spellcrafter and witchcraft practitioner. You can also use such tools in your journey toward becoming a real maker of spells.

Essential Tools for Spellcrafting

To give you an idea, here are some useful tools for spellcrafting and spellcasting.

Athame

Athame refers to a dagger or knife that you can use for ritual purposes. It is conventionally a double-bladed knife that features a black handle. You should never use it for cutting anything, though. It should be exclusive for directing your desired energy during your ritual. One example is when commanding and summoning spirits and elementals.

The athame is also classified as a projective tool symbolizing the air when you think about it based on the classical elements' system. You must put it on your altar, specifically on the East side.

Upon deciding on your athame, you can start customizing it using a meaningful symbol. Make sure to choose a symbol that represents you or has a meaning for you. For example, you can draw a pentagram in it or inscribe your name. You can put any symbol you want on the athame, provided it truly has a special meaning for you.

Bell

Another useful tool and instrument that you can use for spellcrafting is the bell. It is a spiritual musical instrument you can play when evoking positive energies, indicating the start or end of various parts of your rituals, or summoning deities or spirits. The sound produced by the bell is sacred, so it will only be useful every time you get into the ritual mental state.

You can also find those who use Tibetan drums or bowls in place of the bell. One reason behind using such instruments is that it helps create an action in the world that is different from your daily actions.

Broom

While there are legends about flying witches riding on their brooms, the one you can use in crafting spells and your rituals is a misunderstood magical instrument. Contrary to what others believe (that it is a bad instrument used by witches), the main purpose of the broom that we are talking about here is to clean only.

Note, though, that you can't use it for cleaning materially or physically. What it is going to clean is the energy. It works in purifying your sacred environment before the actual opening of the circle.

Due to its purifying and cleaning purposes, many associate it with the water element. You can also use it in love spells as well as spells designed to improve your psychic powers. Many practitioners also believe that hanging a broom behind a door can help protect a house from negativity and evil spells.

Traditionally, you need to use the actual broom but note that you can also make your own. Use ash to create the stick, then tie broom or birch branches together with the help of a willow.

Wand

When directing energies, you can also use the wand – which is an invocation instrument. It symbolizes the air element and must be around 15 to 20 inches long. The wand can also be made using any type of wood, including willow, oak, peach, and cherry.

Certain versions of wands are also constructed from crystal, metal, or stone. The material used in creating the wand will depend on the specific purpose for which you intend to use it. It would be best to use the wand for your spells and rituals during the spring, specifically at sunset or dawn or at midnight or noon every Wednesday.

Cauldron

The cauldron is a symbol of water and the Goddess. Traditionally, it should use iron material for its construction and should be around three feet on its base. The cauldron should also have a narrower opening compared to the rest of its body.

If your cauldron is small enough, it would be a great instrument for ritual cooking and for cooking herbal teas. The cauldron also seems to serve another role or purpose when placed on your altar. When performing spring rituals, for instance, you can fill it up with flowers and water.

It is, therefore, safe to assume that the cauldron serves as a valuable container for every consecrated object. You can also use it as a container for your burnt offerings to the gods.

You need to light up a small fire inside the cauldron during winter rituals. Just be cautious whenever you decide to burn or light up something in the cauldron to guarantee your safety.

Chalice

The chalice refers to a cup that features a long stem. You can fill up the chalice with a wide range of liquids every time you perform rituals or cast spells. In most cases, the chalice is meant to hold water, the element represented by the tool, which has to be on the altar all the time.

Aside from that, the chalice is also a tool you can use to pour wine during ritual toasts and Sabbat offerings, as well as blood and other liquid forms based on what exact spell you intend to make or cast. It is also possible to use a chalice to mix salt and water, so you can trace not only the protective circle but also purifications and blessings.

The chalice useful in spellcrafting and casting is constructed from different materials – among which are brass, silver, ceramic, stone, and glass. You can pick any of the materials you want your chalice to be based on.

Several groups in Wiccan tradition also hold two chalices – one used for cleaning water while the other for the wine and any other form of liquid. When in a coven, you need a main chalice that you can carry into the altar to allow consecrations. You must also share this cup with every member during the ceremony.

Some Wiccans also make it a point to garnish the chalices they are using with symbols or runes for decorating purposes. Others also paint the chalice or attach a semi-precious stone. That way, it will begin containing and providing energy to any liquid that's within the chalice.

Candles

You also need candles; many practitioners consider these as having an extremely vital role in rituals. One reason is that these candles can help create the best state of mind. The color, presence, and aroma of candles work to put you in a good mood.

What's great about choosing the perfect candles for your spells is that they can encourage feelings of love, prosperity, and health. Make it a point to store several candles of any color at home. That way, you no longer have to spend much time looking for a candle before casting your spells.

Altar

The look of the altar does not matter that much in most cases. The most important thing here is the base material, which has to be based on metal or wood. It is also important to set it up so that it contains everything you need for the spell or ritual.

Once you have an altar, prepare a cloth that comes in a color that perfectly suits the ritual or spell you intend to perform. You can then use it as a covering for your altar. Moreover, you should put the Gods' symbols on your altar.

For instance, you can put on a white and black candle to symbolize the mother and father, respectively. Other items you can put on the altar are the wand, bell, cauldron, athame, censer, and any other material or offering for the rite.

Libation Bowl

The libation bowl refers to a dedicated container that you can use to hold a libation, a drink or beverage you can pour out as an offering to the spirit, beloved dead, and deity in a ritual context. One thing to note about libations is that they differ based on traditions.

You can even classify alcoholic beverages, oil, water, honey, and milk as libations. Once inside the libation bowl, it is safe to use it for pouring the drink so you can start offering it to the appropriate spirits and deities.

Scrying Bowl

Scrying is the primary divination strategy that a lot of people are already aware of. It is an ancient divination art with the primary goal of gaining information. You can also often achieve the best results from scrying just by gazing upon or into a reflective surface or a crystal. Let your eyes relax as you gaze into the objects.

Let your inner psychic open so it can receive the information and visions you desire. With the help of scrying tools, like the scrying bowl, you have a higher chance of attaining the mental state needed to enter a trance, serving as the focal point of visualization. You can also use other tools you can see here, like mirrors, polished precious stones, water, and crystal balls.

Cord/Thread

You may also want to use a cord or thread when planning to work with knot magic. Along with the cord and thread, ribbons and strings are primary ingredients in creating and casting knot magic, a process that requires you to tie or bind together.

You may also use black thread in making dolls in other traditions. Moreover, thread is a big help in sewing mojo bags by hand. This will let you create mojo bags that you can also transform into an amulet.

Incense Charcoal

Charcoal refers to the safest and easiest way of burning incense. Use it in cleansing your home. It is ideal for use along with frankincense, palo santo, loose white sage, and copal. After each use, be prepared to handle a lot of ash, but you can rest assured that you can easily dispose of them.

Pentacle

The pentacle is characterized by a 5-pointed star within a circle representing the Earth. It is a protective and evocative tool for spellcrafting and witchcraft, designed to keep your place protected from any form of harm while removing negativity. You can hang this pentacle on your window or doors to protect yourself from any negative energy when performing a ritual. It is also helpful in evoking positive energies. To make the most out of the pentacle, it would be best to bless and consecrate it before each use.

How to Cleanse and Consecrate Magical Tools?

Before using your ritual tools for your spells and rituals, it would be best to customize, cleanse and consecrate them. The process of personalizing, cleansing, and consecrating your tools is even more significant if your ritual tools are purchased instead of being created by you.

The consecration and cleansing process is necessary because it purifies your magical tools before you use them for interacting with the divine. Aside from that, it helps in getting rid of all negative energies that are in the tool. It comes in handy if you are unsure of the past history of the tool or the previous owner before you get a hold of it.

Cleansing

Cleansing your magical tools, as its name suggests, is all about cleaning and purifying them. However, it is also different in the sense that you will not be cleaning the item physically. What you will be doing here is to clean it spiritually, meaning based on its current energy level.

With the help of cleansing, you can disassociate the tools or items used for your magic and spells from their previous vibrations. Note that all the activities that the items went through cause them to collect bits of energy. It could be from when it was still sitting in a store or factory, in transport, sitting on a shelf, or being handled by people.

When the tool reaches you, you may want to focus on wiping its vibrational slate clean. This is so you can keep it attuned to the specific energies you are emitting or the ones that align with your goal.

To cleanse the magical tool/object, follow these simple steps.

- Prepare a cleansing incense – One example is sage. Once you have this incense around, you should burn it, then run the tool through the smoke emitted by the incense.

- After that, bury the tool for a while – Burying the tool in the earth or a bowl containing cornmeal, salt, or dirt will work for that purpose.

- Prepare saltwater – Soak the tool in it. You may also spray or sprinkle your magical tool with salt water.

- Hold the tool for a short period beneath running water – Wave the tool over the flame emitted by a candle, then put it into the fire.

- Use a blessed broom (besom) to sweep away all negative energies.

When doing the steps, you have to be cautious and practical. Be extra careful when following the steps and ensure that what you are doing perfectly fits the material you are cleansing and handling. For instance, if your magical tool is made of metal, you should avoid soaking it in saltwater overnight; otherwise, it will risk developing rust. Also, avoid putting a fabric pouch containing several herbs close to a fire.

Use your sense of judgment whenever you are cleansing to guarantee your safety. Aim to do the process of cleansing new magical tools before using them for rituals and other spiritual purposes or cleansing already existing tools, like crystals, altar tools, and jewelry, especially if you are using them a lot, while prioritizing your safety. Cleansing is also necessary for magical and spellcrafters tools that sit unused for a long time.

Consecrating

After cleansing, you should consecrate your magical tools. The consecration process is all about making your magical tools sacred using minor acts of blessing or rites. It requires you to elevate the purpose of your magical tools into a spiritual one by performing the art of blessing. Any tool you intend to use is suitable for consecration, including jewelry items and other tools. You can even consecrate the ground beneath your house.

Note, though, that once you consecrate the tool, you should start treating it accordingly, as it is already sacred. Some steps you should take when consecrating an item are indicated next.

- Say a prayer over the magical tool. Dedicate your use of it to the Gods and its intended purpose.

- Use cleansed, consecrated, and charged oils to anoint your magical tool/s.

- Consecrate the tool using the elements of earth, water, fire, and air when performing a blessing ritual – What you should do is run the tool through the smoke of incense. Have some salt sprinkled on it, then let the tool pass through the flame. After that, sprinkle some water on it.

- Increase the tool's intent to perform the good work executed by the abundant universe.

Charging

Apart from cleansing and consecrating, you may also want to add the crucial process of charging your magical tools. When you charge your tools, you mainly empower them with appropriate energy. You may want to imbue the tools with positivity or have them charged in such a way that their vibrations start to become aligned with a certain intention.

Charging requires you to raise your own level of energy to direct it to your magical tools. You can choose a charging method based on what you prefer and the specific tool/s you are charging.

Here are some effective methods of charging your spellcrafter and magical tools.

- Dancing, chanting, or meditating – This should help raise the tool's power and then pour such energy imaginatively into it using a song, targeted or focused intent, or movement.

- Doing a small ritual should aim to increase energy and intent while keeping you invested in your item.

- Performing visualization – This helps transmit intent and energy to your tools, after which you can release them so that the tool can perform its intended function.

Note that you can also develop something that is only yours. You can create it in such a way that you can accomplish your goal based on your belief system.

Basic Layout for your Altar

The altar is the focal point of all your spellwork and rituals. This means that it is unique since it is going to be you who will design and customize it based on your personality and the spells you intend to make and cast. Also, note that from one witch, ritual, and even spell to another, it is highly likely for the altar to be dynamic. It changes all the time. This is what makes the altar remain alive and keeps the energy flowing.

Therefore, the altar's layout - while having basic components - is going to be up to the witchcraft practitioner. Also, note that your main purpose for practicing can greatly affect the entire layout, shape, and size.

It is easy and simple to set up a basic altar. It often just requires any table where you can put the tools you intend to use and the symbols that depict your beliefs. An important rule is to feel free to explore, decorate, redecorate/rearrange the components of your altar. Do not forget to have fun while creating or setting up your altar.

Before putting an item on the altar, make sure that you study its meaning first. Also, reflect on the specific reasons why you like to use the item or tool and how to use it effectively. Avoid cluttering your altar, too. Remember that your altar also serves as your workspace, so there should be enough room and space for all your tools and ingredients.

Make it a point to empty it when unused. Do not clutter it by setting an actual place for you to put and organize your tools. It could be on a shelf, box, or drawer – anywhere you can safely put them away.

Decorating Your Altar

To give you an idea of how you can lay out and decorate your altar, we are going to talk about its most common components.

Altar Cloth

Regardless of the altar you intend to create, you should cover the surface with a cloth. This should serve as an ornamental piece that protects the table from scratches, wax drippings, and liquids. Shop for a cloth that you can use for your altar. If there is one that catches your interest that also has a symbol in it, inquire about the actual meaning.

Find out if it is truly meaningful for you before buying it and using it on your altar. If you are up to it, you can also make your cloth. You can change the cloth based on the kind of ritual you intend to do. The changes may depend on the season and the Pagan holiday you are celebrating.

Religious Symbols

You may want to put some religious symbols on your altar if you are a practitioner who strongly connects to Hinduism, Buddhism, Christianity, or any other spiritual tradition. In this case, you may put some figures and images symbolizing your beliefs that also remind you of who you really are.

Are you devoted to a certain deity? Then you may also put a drawing or statue symbolizing that deity on your altar. If you consider yourself a Wiccan, you can put a pentagram in the middle of the altar.

Candle Holder

You need the candle holder as part of your altar decoration if you have plans to work with candle magic. Ensure that you have at least one of these holders. Your choice of a candle holder also needs to be strong and sturdy enough to withstand the candle's heat without easily falling over in case you accidentally bump into the altar. Choose eco-friendly and biodegradable tools, too. Among the best materials for the candle holder are glass, metal, and ceramics.

Incense Burner

The incense burner is also important for your altar if you intend to cast a spell. This burner is available in several styles and shapes. You may also put a cauldron on the altar to let you burn some herbs for your spells and rituals.

Creating the Altar

Based on the mentioned components, note that the altar has building blocks in the form of its four traditional elements – all of which you can align with the help of four cardinal points. As an example, here is a layout of a basic altar that spellcrafters use.

- A bowl containing sand, plant, or dirt is positioned on the altar's North end– This should represent the earth element.

- Stick of incense – Put it in the East to symbolize the air element.

- Charcoal or candle – Position it in the South to represent the fire element.

- Bowl or glass with water – Make sure it faces the east to represent the water element.

Light the candle and incense every time you need to craft or cast spells or during rituals. Be extra careful, though. Never leave burning candles behind without you around. In case you need to go somewhere, blow it out.

Chapter 4 – Getting Started with Ritual

Now, it is time for you to start your spells and rituals. Before starting, you should remember how serious each spell or ritual is. You need to be prepared for it physically and mentally, so if you are still underaged or someone who is still battling with a mental health issue, you have to avoid it.

If you are fully certain you can handle the spellwork and ritual, you should start preparing for it. Remember that unless you prepare for it properly and appropriately, it will be impossible for you to make it produce the result you want. You must do meticulous preparation while adhering to instructions to ensure that your rituals and spells will work based on how you intend them to.

Selecting the Perfect Ritual Location

One of the first things you should do when preparing for the spellcrafting ritual is the location. It serves as your magic space where you can hold your ritual, so select this space carefully. You need the right location for your ritual as it contributes greatly to attaining your intended result.

Pick a space that has a certain calm. It should be a place that will not disturb you in any way, especially when you are either crafting or casting your spells. Note, though, that you still have to plan for any unexpected interruptions in advance, so you will know what to do in case those come, no matter how careful you are.

The ideal ritual location is outdoors. It should be in a quiet and natural environment that is close to the earth. It could be in a meadow, field, forest, or any location that is close to the water or trees.

However, keep in mind that you will be unable to hold the ritual outdoors all the time. The most convenient place would still be in your home. In that case, look for a spot in your home with sufficient calmness and quietness. It should let you hold your rituals without any disturbance. Moreover, it needs to have sufficient space so you can cast the circle needed for all forms of ritual.

Cleansing your Magical or Sacred Space

Once you have chosen your ritual space, it is time to cleanse it. Cleansing is necessary before crafting and casting any spell, as it will help rid your space of negative vibrations and energies. The good news is that there are many ways for you to do the cleansing – some of which will be discussed briefly next.

Ritual

This cleansing method requires using rock salt, four white fabric bags, and sea salt. Mix the salts, then put the mixture inside the bags. Put each bag in every corner of your sacred space so you can completely cleanse it. While putting the bag, say this spell.

I am cleansing this sacred space

I am commanding every negative force and vibration

To get out of this place

So mote it be

Visualize the negative energies and vibrations leaving your sacred or magical space while you say the statement. You may also smudge this space using sage.

Smudging

For this specific cleansing method, you will need a smudge stick. In this case, the most suitable for use are sweetgrass, sage, frankincense, and cedar. Here are the steps for using the smudge stick.

- Light the smudge stick – Continue lighting it until it burns – after which you should blow it out. Expect the stick to continue producing smoke, which is what you should aim for.

- Walk starting in the east – This means walking the whole space following a clockwise motion starting from the east. Your goal here is to smudge the entire space.

- Visualize all the negative vibrations and energies leaving your sacred space as you do the smudging.

Sweeping

The simple act of sweeping your entire space is also an effective way to cleanse your sacred space. This requires the use of the besom or broom, which is specifically designed for magical uses.

- Sweep your entire sacred space – Begin in the east and do it clockwise.

- Clean the air symbolically – To do that, just lift the besom as high as possible.

- As you sweep, visualize the negative vibrations and energies finally saying goodbye from your space.

Cleansing Yourself

Apart from your sacred space, you must also cleanse yourself in preparation for the ritual. Spend time before the ritual to choose a special bath salt, herbal bath, or soap for the pre-ritual cleansing. It is unnecessary to take the cleansing bath before the actual ritual if you do not prefer to do so. Doing it one night before is okay if you think it fits better with your lifestyle and schedule.

When preparing for the cleansing bath, note that you are also allowed to select the ornaments. You can add candles to the area. You may also pour a few drops of your chosen essential oils into the water you will use.

If you have crystals, you can also put them around your bathtub. Be extra cautious when using crystals around water, though. The reason is that some of them, such as lapis lazuli, kyanite, malachite, and selenite, should never be directly exposed to salt water or pure water. If you wish to use the crystals for your cleansing bath, study them first to guarantee your safety.

In addition to the spiritual cleansing ritual bath that you can do by taking a bath in water that you infuse with flowers, salts, teas, crystal vibrations, herbs, and crystals, among many others, you may also choose to do self-cleansing rituals using other means.

- Smudging Ritual – This requires you to use the smoke that comes out of certain herbs so you can cleanse your aura. Among the herbs you can use for this self-cleansing smudging ritual are sweetgrass, cedar, sage, palo santo, and rosemary.

- Crystal Ritual – Here, you will need to use a wand with a high-vibrational crystal, like selenite. You should let the wand pass over your body to remove all negative vibrations and energies.

- Asperging (blessing) using blessed or holy water – This method requires you to spray or spritz the blessed or holy water over your body. Make sure that you cover each part of yourself, from your head down to your feet. Aside from the actual holy water, you may also use rose water and moon water, among others.

- Energetic cleansing – This requires the use of divine healing energies, like Reiki, to cleanse yourself.

Another method, though not highly recommended as it involves the use of fire that may lead to accidents if you are not careful, is bonfire cleansing. It is a ritual that requires you to pass through a couple of bonfires or leap over one to have yourself cleansed.

Wearing Appropriate Colors

Preparing for the ritual also involves wearing the appropriate colors for it. Note that color energy will always be a vital aspect of every ritual work, so you should make it a part of your preparation. Pick clothing or any other adornment depending on the kind of energy you intend to create in your sacred space. Take a look at these colors to guide you.

- Black – designed for transformation and the releasing and banishing of negative energies

- White - understanding, cleansing, finding clarity, building order, spiritual growth
- Orange - power and encouragement
- Red - health rituals and love spells
- Blue - intensifying psychic abilities and healing rituals
- Green - good luck, prosperity, money spells, employment spells, and fertility rituals
- Yellow - divination and communication spells
- Brown - home rituals, grounding and balance
- Violet - balance and divination
- Gray - complex decision-making and binding any negative influence
- Silver - meditation, the release of negativity, psychic development
- Pink - romance and love spells, kid's magic, and spiritual awakening
- Gold - divination, spells for good fortune, success, and health
- Indigo - meditation and spiritual healing

In addition to the color of your clothing, it is also advisable to use freshly washed and clean ones. Remember that you may be staying in an awkward or unusual pose when performing the ritual for a prolonged period, so choose comfortable clothing that blends well with the present weather.

Gathering the Right Materials

Another important thing to do is to use the best materials that are the most appropriate for the spell you intend to make. Note that various oils, herbs, and candles may be necessary to effectively execute the ritual or spell. The spell's progress may get damaged if you use inappropriate and incorrect materials.

Every ingredient also possesses certain power and energy that works specifically for your goal. Yes, indeed, advanced practitioners are already skilled enough that they can substitute certain materials and ingredients. However, since you are still a beginner, it is not advisable to do so. Make it a point to get the right materials, prepare them for the ritual, and spell appropriately.

Once you have gathered the materials needed for your spell, start setting them out depending on the specific manner through which they are guaranteed to work. For instance, if you use certain candles, you may have to use a special oil first to anoint them. It may also be necessary to put the candles in a specific formation to radiate the correct energy.

If you are using herbs, you may have to burn or consume them in a specific way that helps harness their full potency. For tools and crystals, cleansing and charging them may be necessary. You can do all the steps necessary to prepare your materials during the planning stage. By doing that, you are assured that every material and tool you need is ready for what's ahead once it is time to perform the actual ritual or spell.

Preparing your Mental State

Another important aspect of ritual preparation is your mental state. You have to keep yourself attuned to the ritual since it will be you who has the primary role in the process. This is where you should remind yourself that you should avoid holding rituals, crafting spells, casting spells, or performing any other magical work in case you are experiencing some issues affecting your mental state.

It could be that you feel unwell or sick, or you are mentally unstable or emotionally agitated, probably because of anger and grief. It could also be that your intuition is telling you that you should not do the ritual or magical work at that particular time. In that particular case, you have to listen to what your intuition is telling you.

You may also want to follow the technique of other spellcasters and witches who tend to fast before performing the ritual. They do so as they feel like it will be a big help in internally cleansing themselves, thereby keeping them free as much as possible.

You should also avoid drinking alcohol or using any drug or unwanted substances 12 hours or so before the scheduled ritual. The goal here is to keep your mind as clear as possible so you can bring it to its absolute peak as far as its strength is concerned.

It is also advisable to spend at least half an hour preparing yourself mentally before the actual ritual. Look at yourself internally. Focus on yourself and the ritual or magical work you are about to execute. Ensure that you are clear regarding what you want from the ritual and how you intend it to work.

Aside from that, set yourself free from all the things that bother and hinder you. Give yourself the kind of internal purification that you need. Imagine the dissipation of all your negative energies and influences, including your anger and stress.

You should then make room for the coming of the white flame that tends to burn brightly inside you. Once you feel like you are already calm, relaxed, and strong, then you are truly prepared to begin and do your ritual.

How to Cast the Circle

The circle we are talking about here frequently refers to a barrier that houses your rituals and spells. You need to cast this circle before your rituals and spells to ensure that you have allocated more than enough energy to protect yourself from negative and unwanted outside influences. The good thing about casting a circle is that you can do it in many ways – some are formal, while others are informal.

Traditionally, casting a circle may involve calling upon a goddess or a god. However, suppose you consider yourself a secular witch. What you will most likely be calling upon would be the elements. It is also possible for you to develop a wall composed of your own energy. The circle is extremely important in witchcraft as it can assist with energy and protection.

Remember that casting a circle does not have formal instructions for doing it correctly. You can use a wide range of tools for this purpose as you see fit. These include candles, crystals, flowers, twigs, herbs, and ropes. However, if you are still a beginner and looking for an idea to cast the circle and use it as your guide, here is a simple technique you can adhere to. You may modify it as you deem fit.

- Clear your sacred space from clutter – Ensure that there will be no source of disturbance as you cast the circle and perform your ritual afterward.

- Prepare four candles – Light them up, then arrange them based on the four cardinal directions – North (earth), South (fire), East (air), and West (water). The candle arrangement should have a diameter of five to six feet.

- After preparing all the tools you need, start centering yourself – The goal here is to let yourself be in a state of calm that is perfect for meditation. You know that you are ready when you have already achieved a superior state of calmness.

- Once ready, stand while facing the East – When in that position, call upon or summon the air spirits to give you guidance and protection. Do this for the remaining elements.

- Once done with all the elements, affirm by saying, *"I have cast the circle. Blessed be"* – Utilize this specific moment to start meditating or doing magic.

- After the ritual, dissolve the circle – Put off the candles and finish the entire practice with a gratitude heart meant specifically for the divine.

When casting a circle, remember there are no right and wrong steps. Similar to other similar practices, you must commit to applying your creativity and intuition in the practice. Make sure that you do whatever it is that you feel is right. Just don't forget to stick to the most important rule when casting the circle, which is the direction of the energy.

The Rule of Three (The Threefold Law)

Once you have successfully cast the circle, you can cast your spells or perform the intended ritual safely. When it is time for you to perform the magical ritual or work, you should never deviate from the ultimate Rule of Three, also called the Threefold Law or Law of Threefold Return.

This is an important rule/law in witchcraft as this requires you to follow the principle of avoiding the act of casting spells or performing rituals that aim to cause harm to someone or something. The reason is that if you do so, it will only activate bad karma, which is otherwise referred to by the witches as the Rule of Three.

This rule is a religious tenet that many Wiccans, occultists, and neo-pagans hold onto. Here, you will have to remind yourself all the time that whatever energy you release to the world, whether it is positive or negative, may go back to you threefold. Because of this principle, it is no longer surprising to see Wiccans describing this law as karma.

Based on some traditions, the threefold law or rule of three is not completely literal. However, it represents the fact that your energy will go your way again as many times as possible for you to learn and understand all the lessons linked to it. This is why you must be extra careful when performing rituals and crafting spells.

You have to be one hundred percent sure that it will never cause any harm to anyone, so you can avoid ruining yourself with your bad karma.

Chapter 5 – Protection and Defense Spells

You can't avoid stress and danger all the time. No matter how careful you are, there will still be several instances when you will feel stressed out and in danger. The problem is that any feeling of being unsafe or in danger, whether spiritually, physically, or emotionally, may sap your energy and cause your entire wellbeing to be overly strained.

Fortunately, you can now handle that feeling of being in danger with the aid of protection spells. These spells will be of great help whether you just want to improve your emotional wellbeing or your stability, no matter how stressful – and sometimes dangerous – the world is.

With the help of protection spells, you can give yourself a strong defense and protection from harm, stress, and bad energies and your family and your loved ones. The protection spells can also help you ward off toxic and unpleasant people, eliminate unhealthy influences, and protect everything that belongs to you.

Importance of Protection Spells

For the protection spell to affect change, you need to do it with a high level of focus and intent. Every time you craft spells and finally cast them, you serve as the agent whose goal is to activate change. You will be the one to direct and form energy to your preferred outcome.

Since what you will be focusing on are the defense and protection spells and magic, expect them to work based on a certain set of intentions guaranteed to help in cleansing and getting rid of negativity.

Spells specifically meant to give you protection also have multiple facets. You can use them to protect someone or something from negative energy, defend yourself from an attack, and protect someone else or yourself from certain harm or danger. This type of spell is also important as it helps maintain a general defense level.

Protection spells are also important as they can make you feel personally and professionally protected. You can even use these spells as protection from possible harassment and bullying in the workplace. Anything that may cause permanent damage to your life can be dealt with by making protection spells and casting them at the right time.

The spells may also be useful in protecting your partner's integrity and keeping your relationship strong. This is possible as you can use the spells to avoid external forces that may interfere with your loving and secure relationship.

One more thing that protection spells can do is protect your wealth and health. You will no longer feel afraid when activating your protection shield through the spells, even when walking in harmful and dangerous situations.

You will feel at ease knowing you have a defense from anything and anyone that may harm or hurt you. The protection spells can give you a shielding layer that will encourage you to handle serious situations confidently.

As a guide to this type of spell, the first thing you will most likely have to do is cleanse your space as well as the tools you intend to use. Be clear on your intent, too. This means that you should clarify whatever you wish to achieve from the spell.

Visualizing your preferred outcome should come next. After that, you can do the exact steps for your ritual. End this process by expressing your gratitude.

Types of Protection Spells

Protection spells come in different forms and types. This means you can just pick one based on the kind and level of defense you would like to give yourself.

Basic Shield Protection

You can use this kind of protection spell anytime you feel like you need a basic shield or defense from harm. To do it, keep yourself centered first, then ground your energy. You can do the grounding if you take seven deep breaths. Imagine drawing up the energy from the Earth to your core as you take in each breath.

After that, visualize the energy as it extends past your core and expands as a means of creating a physical bubble surrounding you. You may look at the energy as something that resembles a soap bubble that slowly and gently encircles your whole body. If you want, you can expand the bubble even further if what you intend to encircle with the shield of protection is your whole apartment or house.

Secure the visualization by changing a protection spell – the one you crafted, preferably. The spell could be stated this way.

"I summon/invoke this shield of protection

Nothing can ail me or put me in danger while I am encircled in this magical protection."

Protection Charm

You can also create a protection charm that you can use to improve the results of your spells. It is okay to carry this charm with you all the time. You may use a piece of jewelry you already have at home and just add magic. Once enchanted, you can then wear the charm anytime and anywhere.

You may also want to buy a new jewelry piece specifically designed for protection. Let the jewelry pass through the smoke of incense to cleanse it first. You may also do the cleansing by doing a suitable ritual that you have chosen.

To use a protection charm for your spells, you must gather the following items.

- One incense stick – You may also use a bundle of smoke-cleansing herbs.
- Lighter or match
- A piece of jewelry

Here are the steps in taking advantage of this protection charm and spell.

- Cleanse your space. After that, you should define your intention. It should be clear enough to avoid confusion when trying to draw positive energy and drive negative ones away. Ground your energy right after.

- Use the lighter or match to light up the herb bundle or incense. Let the piece of jewelry pass through the smoke – after which, say this spell or another one with the same meaning as this one.

"By the power carried by this purifying and cleansing smoke

I am now cleansing you of every negative and unwanted energy."

- Hold the piece of jewelry using your hands. Imagine the earth's energy flowing up. Let it fill your core.

- Direct the flowing energy to the piece of jewelry, then say the following,

"I am charging this item

To serve as my shield, keeping me protected from danger and injury."

After that, the charm will be ready for use. Start wearing it anywhere you go to serve as your ultimate source of protection from harm.

Purifying Bath Protection Spell

This specific protection spell ritual is very beautiful and magical, as you can use it to cleanse not only your space but also your spirit. This type of spell anytime you feel like what you need is more than the usual quick fix. The good thing about the purifying bath is that it can help you relax deeply and make you feel comfortable.

Expect this ritual to focus on removing negative energies, so you can surround yourself with the protective shield. You may be able to find additional herbs and oils that you can use for this bath protection spell in your kitchen or pantry. Basically, though, the things you need for this spell are one cup of Epsom salt, three drops of sandalwood essential oil, and one teaspoon of dried rosemary.

- Mix the mentioned ingredients in a tiny bowl.

- Set an intention – The intention you can set could be in this line or anything similar, *"I am completely relaxed, comfortable, and protected."*

- Prepare the bath -Sstart sprinkling the Epsom salt blend beneath running water.

- Visualize the intention while letting yourself soak in the bath. Continue soaking for as long as possible - Once done, imagine every negative energy coming down together with the prepared bathwater.

One thing to note when creating this type of protection is that unlike all the other forms of spellwork, you should specifically focus on the protection's intent for rituals and spells. This should help you attain the best results.

Protective Amulets and Talismans

Talismans and amulets are built for certain purposes - one of which is protection. The two work together by immediately influencing the energy surrounding them, which is why you can see them being worn and carried frequently or positioned in an area's entryway or a central location.

A major difference is that a talisman focuses more on the signs and symbols used in creating it. You can choose certain protective symbols and allow them to work into the piece.

On the other hand, the amulet is mainly designed for your chosen and used materials. This means you can choose the items and materials for your spells and rituals and then direct their positive energies to the amulet by working them into the piece. Note, though, that you are allowed to combine the mentioned focuses. You can refer to the result as either a talisman, amulet, or just a charm, thereby covering each base.

Apart from protection, you can also use amulets and talismans for various purposes. You can create them to draw love, employment, or money. You can also make the talismans hold sigils or symbols that can help in attracting specific kinds of spiritual beings. You can use it mainly to protect yourself or perform other purposes.

To let you know about the protective symbols or sigils you can incorporate into your talismans, here is a list of some of them.

- Mars symbol - Generally, the energy emitted by Mars is protective, so you may want to use the symbol of this planet. You can use this as a sigil to protect you from possible accidents and stolen and lost damage, especially if you travel often.

- Pentagram - This one is also a generally protective symbol. You can use it to defend yourself from spiritual and psychic intrusion.

- Eye images and Hamsa - You can use this symbol to gain protection from the evil eye.

- Cross - It is a protective symbol for malignant spirits. It is ideal for you if you are following a suitable belief system.

- Janus image - It should protect locations, especially if you put it on the entryways.

- Crossed weapons - Any crossed weapons, like spears, symbolize the guardians who tend to block the way of those who are only looking for trouble.

- Eye of Horus - You will find this symbol useful when trying to protect yourself and your family from evil.

- Brigid's cross - This symbol is useful in keeping your home or any other property from fire and lighting.

Note that you can use bind runes and sigils to develop your protective symbols. Once you already have a protective amulet, talisman, or symbol, you can start bringing it with you anywhere or making it a part of your rituals and spells by ensuring that you also put it on the altar.

Casting a Circle of Protection

Probably the most effective and common form of protection ritual that you can use right now is the casting of the circle. As mentioned in the previous chapter, the circle is definitely one of the most valuable components of a ritual or spell. It is even more valuable when used for protection.

You may want to cast a circle of protection to ensure that you are fully protected whenever you perform magical work. When casting a protective circle, remember that you will need a space with a high level of energy. It should be a spot that will let you execute and perform magic safely without being interrupted by any harmful entity that may otherwise get attracted by the metaphysical energies that you possess during your spellcasting and rituals.

The first thing that you should do here is to mark out the circle. Make sure you are already fully aware of the exact spot where you can create the circle. Regardless of if you are doing the ritual or spell on an altar or any other part of your home or outdoors, pick a spot for the circle that will keep you undisturbed. That way, you can peacefully focus and work on your magic and ritual.

Use a long cord to mark the circle's boundaries. Alternatively, you can put some rocks or candles along all the edges. You can also use crystals that can provide additional protection to the circle.

Once marked, you can start conjuring pure energy capable of surrounding and protecting you. The good news is that there are several ways to do it, so you can rest assured that there is one that perfectly suits you as well as your practices.

Basic Circle of Protection

Casting this basic circle of protection is quick and easy as it does not involve using tools. Just follow the steps below.

- After marking out the circle, stand in the middle of it. Allow yourself to relax and practice deep breathing - Visualize your crown (top of the head) opening up like a funnel receiving the white and divine light. Note that the crown will always be connected to your higher self and the divine. This means that opening it up and amplifying this particular channel is possible based on your will.

- Open your arms - Your palms should also be facing out when doing this. As you take in each breath, imagine that you are pulling down the divine and pure light through the crown. Channel out the light every time you breathe out. You can do that through your palms. This should help in letting a protective shield surround you.

- Allow the high-vibration energy to fill the entire space surrounding you - When that happens, expect to experience a buzzing or tingling feeling. It may cause you to have goosebumps, or you may enjoy a light and uplifting feeling.

- Hold one outstretched arm - Point this arm to the circle's edge. Spin clockwise thrice, mentally allowing the divine light to mark out the circle. After that, lift both your arms over your head, then say something like this,

"I summon the presence of the God and Goddess
With your power and grace, bless this circle
To keep me free, safe, and protected inside this sacred space
So mote it be."

Once you have said that, it indicates that you are already ready to perform the ritual or cast the spell. Close the circle properly upon the end of the ritual. Do that by holding your arm out and then spinning it around in an anti-clockwise motion thrice. You should then feel the dispersion of the protective and divine light. Do not forget to thank the spirits for being present before declaring the circle closed.

Advanced Circle of Protection

If you prefer to do a more advanced version of the circle of protection, then you can use this one as a guide. Here, you will need one compass and four candles. You may also want to use a wand or athame to direct energy. The candles could be white or colored and should represent each point or direction.

- North – green
- South – red
- East – yellow
- West – blue

Make use of the compass, then put each candle on every cardinal point. As you put and light each candle, say this one (make sure that you change the cardinal point and the represented element every time).

"Guardians of the (state the cardinal point or direction)

Element of the (state the represented element – earth for the north, air for the east, fire for the south, and water for the west)

I summon/invoke your presence during this ritual

Please be with me in my ritual and bless this circle."

Once you have finished lighting the candles in all cardinal points and directions, take your athame or wand. You should point this magical tool to the circle's edge. Spin around in a clockwise motion thrice.

After that, visualize a white and bright light penetrating your crown. Use either the athame or wand to direct such light out. It should be through your arm, then the tool, and then out. This should help in forming the circle's edge.

The next step is standing in the middle of the circle. Feel the white and divine light as it fills the circle and immerses your whole being. Say this during that stage.

"Guardian angels, spirit guides, and Gods and Goddesses

I summon/invoke your presence during this ritual

Grace this circle with your blessing, and help me stay protected

I forbid unwanted entities from entering this circle

Only divine and pure beings can enter my sacred space

I hereby cast the circle

So mote it be."

This should prompt your readiness to execute the ritual or cast your spell. After that, close the circle with the help of your athame or wand. Just spin this tool around in an anti-clockwise motion thrice, then feel and notice the dispersing of the protective light. Do not forget to thank the presence of elements and spirits. End this ritual by announcing the closing of the circle.

Chapter 6 – Magic Herbs and Plants

Plant magic is an old tradition that you can trace back to the ancient times of the Egyptians. When talking about plant magic, note that it involves using herbs and plants known for possessing magical powers and energies for a wide range of purposes - healing, protection, love spells, and self-empowerment.

Every plant or herb possesses magical properties, powers, and strengths, so you can use them to increase the power of your spells. If you use them, you can rest assured that you have a higher chance of attaining your desired results regardless of your level of strength as the crafter and caster of the spell.

The reason is that plants and herbs already contain many magical properties. The fact that plant magic has a lot of uses, not to mention being effective and having the ability to produce quick results, indicates its popularity among a lot of witchcraft practitioners until today.

How to Use Magic Herbs and Plants?

With the proven powers and magical properties of herbs and plants, you will notice that they are not only used by witches for healing. You can also see these plants being used in alternative medicines, as well as in food and health supplements and dietary products.

When it comes to using them for your spells, though, the best method would be sprinkling some herbs into a candle flame while performing your ritual. By doing that, you can make your spells more powerful.

You can also find other ways to make plants and herbs a part of your spell work and rituals. The good news is that most of these methods are easy and quick to do.

- Mix them and visualize their results and effects - This is an effective tip when it comes to making herbs a part of your spell. By doing this, you can pass on the magical properties, powers, and energies of the herbs to your spell. This can make your spell stronger and more vigorous.

- Roll anointed or oiled candles into your chosen herb or herb mixture - This simple technique works in transmitting the energies of the herbs to the anointed or oiled candles. The energies and powers transmitted to the candles will also be spread to their flame and your spell or ritual.

- Burn your chosen herbs - Burning them in small discs or charcoal blocks is highly recommended.

- Put the herbs of your choice in an incense burner tray made of metal - After that, light the herbs and burn them.

- Burn every sturdy herb you can think of directly - Some examples of these herbs are mugwort, cedar, and sage. These are flammable herbs that it is possible to light them on fire directly.

- Set them on fire - This method is necessary for cleansing. With that said, you can do it in any part of performing the spell. It could be before, during, and after the spell. The magical plants and herbs can help clear away negative energies, thereby preparing you for the spell or ritual. It can also help in getting rid of negative energies brought by the spell to the surface.

- Create potions - You can also use herbs and plants to make magical potions. Once you have these potions, you can start using them in your spells and rituals.

- Create tinctures, oils, herb bags, and incenses – Having these items made of magical herbs and plants around can help you work on your spell or ritual for a long time, usually for a few months at a time. As each spell works, you can also expect the herbal product or essence to add or integrate more energy into it.

When it comes to using magic plants and herbs for your rituals and spells, you should remind yourself that even just a little amount of them can already work wonders. They are so powerful, so even if you start small, you can already get good results. Just add more herbs if necessary. Also, you should never ingest the herbs and plants used for your spells and rituals. The reason is that doing so can only put you in danger.

Another way to take advantage of the magic herbs and plants is to leave a small amount of them in all parts of your home. This should help in getting rid of negative energies surrounding your home and offering you protection. It can also bring happiness and peaceful energy while promoting good health.

Another common practice is carrying a charm bag containing various magical herbs. Bring this charm bag with you all the time so you can enjoy a lot of positive things from it, including love and protection. It is also advisable to do plant magic or gather magical herbs and plants at night. It should preferably be under a full moon as this is the time when they are most powerful.

Herbs and Plants for Spellcrafting and Spellcasting

Now, let's familiarize ourselves with the long list of herbs and plants known for holding a lot of healing and magical properties. With the properties they hold, you have an assurance that they can help raise and enhance the energy of your ritual and spellwork.

Acacia

Also called mimosa, Arabic gum, or wattle, acacia has magick properties that can provide protection against the "evil eye." Bless (or asperge) your candles, censers, and other tools with it; you can also anoint/bless containers holding your magick tools. In addition to aiding in meditation, you can use it in your bathing ritual to ward off bad spells or keep future issues at bay.

Aloe

This fantastic plant is so powerful that it can provide you with not only protection but also luck and fortune. Place it on your loved ones' resting place for peace, or use it in your home to promote luck and protection for those living under your roof.

Want a new lover in your life? Burn aloe at night (and particularly on a full moon), and you can bring a new lover into your life. Some use it to have a former lover return to the nest! In addition to its great uses in the field of magic and witchcraft, this plant is also capable of easing several skin problems.

Amber

This plant is recognized for its ability to protect against many forms of danger, whether it is psychic attacks from within or evil spells/attacks from outside sources. It can promote a high level of focus and mental clarity. It even works in turning negative energies into positive ones. Just avoid consuming the berries of this plant because they are toxic.

Angelica

Powerful protection against many forms of negative energy! Like acacia, sprinkle it around your home, and place it in your bath water. You can add it to your incense burner to help with healing. Again, like the acacia, it's a powerful sort of protection from hexes.

Anise

Similar to Angelica above. Protect yourself from the evil eye. But wait, there's more! This wonderful herb helps with digestion issues as well. After meals, consider drinking star anise tea for help with gas, bloating, and constipation. Also, include it in your spells, use it in incense, and even slip it into your pillowcase to help ward off bad dreams.

Basil

OK, this one is a bit different. Needing more abundance in terms of money? Add hot water to a batch of these powerful leaves, and get to mopping! Need that job? Go sprinkle basil leaves around the bottom of the office building in which you want a job. Or use it around your business structure to attract capital and bring success.

Some wear basil in a necklace/charm/amulet to bring money and prosperity.

Bergamot

Nature's SSRI (antidepressant). Instead of drugs, try this to improve your memory and your sleep! It is also called "Orange Mint."

Black Pepper

Use black pepper before cleansing yourself or your sacred space through smudging or incense. What you should do is burn it so you can eliminate bad, negative, and toxic energies from your household.

You may also want to carry black peppercorns around. This helps banish the evil eye and any feeling of jealousy. Mix black pepper with salt, then scatter this mixture around your home. This should secure your property from any bad and evil energy.

Buckwheat

Buckwheat is also a great partner in your spells and charms. Like many others in this list, use it to attract riches. Need to balance your budget? Put a bowl of buckwheat flour and dried peas somewhere inside your home; don't forget to throw it out once you've reached your goals.

Caraway

The caraway plant has a strong connection to so many positive aspects of life! Use it to bless your ritual tools and protect your home from evil spirits. Some even put this powerful herb under their baby's cradle. Use this plant to bring you good health, increased mental abilities, soaring passion, and loving protection,

You can also use it together with other similar herbs and plants, such as the roots of Angelica.

Cinquefoil

Many consider the cinquefoil a magical one-size-fits-all! Its five-petal ends are representative of five important parts of life: love, power, health, wisdom, and money. You can, therefore, use this herb for a variety of purposes – one of which would be cleansing and blessing your house for protection against bad omens.

You can also create an herb infusion using cinquefoil. Once you have the infusion, wash your forehead and arms with it nine times. This should help in washing out and banishing evil spells and hexes made against you.

Another way to take advantage of the power of this herb is to get an empty eggshell and then fill it up with the cinquefoil. You should then keep it in your home so you can receive protection against evil forces.

Finally, some use red flannel cloth to wrap it up and hang it over sleeping quarters as a way to protect from evil spirits.

Dragon's Blood

Want/need to banish and fight off bad habits or negative influences? Grind Dragon's Blood and sprinkle it around your home to keep you protected from such things.

Eucalyptus

Eucalyptus is also a great magical herb, as it is capable of attracting healing vibrations. It also works incredibly well as far as healing and protection are concerned. Burn eucalyptus, so you can purify your space. You should also carry it with you in the form of an amulet or sachet. Doing this helps in reconciling any difficulty you have with your relationships.

Horehound

How about some mental clarity and enhanced creativity during your spellwork? Horehound also carries properties that promote balance in your personal energy and is perfect for use when you are clearing or blessing your home. Keeping it near doorways is also believed to keep trouble at bay.

Gardenia

Like many other herbs/plants, gardenia is great for warding away evil, strife – and for protecting one's home from such negative outside enemies. Need some peace? Incorporate it into your flower arrangements, incenses, and other healing mixtures.

Garlic

Lots of magical uses for this popular plant. You've surely read stories where it was used in exorcism or to fight off vampires! The lesson here is that this smelly (yet oft-used component of Italian food) has a lot of uses, serving as an effective defense against negative magic, the envy of others, and any sort of spiritual darkness.

Marshmallow Root

It is also a great idea to include a marshmallow root in your spells and rituals. Burning it as incense can promote a higher level of psychic stimulation and protection. You may also want to put a marshmallow root on the altar when performing a ritual. This can help in drawing in and inviting good spirits.

Myrrh

Let's talk about vibrational or spiritual energy; it's the basis for creating change in your life. Myrrh carries a strong connection with vehicles used in reaching such heightened states and also promotes alignment. Use it in incense, add it to charms, or burn it with Frankincense. Yes, just like the Christmas story: the Wise Men brought Frankincense and Myrrh as gifts to baby Jesus.

Quince

Looking for Love? Happiness? Better luck? A "bodyguard" for evil? Look no further! Put some of these powerful seeds in a red flannel bag and say goodbye to physical attacks and harmful circumstances. Use it in your spells and charms to enhance its powers!

St. John's Wort

You can wear this herb as a means of preventing fever and colds. It also works for those who are looking for a sort of protection from black witchcraft. Just put this herb in a jar, then place it in one of your windows. You may also burn St. John's Wort in your fireplace to encourage protection from evil spirits, fire, and lightning.

This chapter covers just a few of the hundreds of magical herbs and plants that you can use to increase the power and potency of your spells. Make them a part of your spells and rituals, and you will surely enjoy their healing properties and get the results you want from your spellwork.

Chapter 7 – Candle Magick Spells

Candles usually have mystical meanings aside from their primary function of providing light. As a matter of fact, candles have been used as primary elements in several magical practices and spells, including Wicca and Pagans. Several magic practitioners also have their individual perspectives and concepts regarding candles.

Generally, candle magic is a simple form of spellcasting. It is simple in that it does not require plenty of fancy ceremonial and ritual tools. This means that even if you only have a candle, you can already cast a spell.

Utilized in spellwork for over 25,000 years, the use of candles is a pure form of sympathetic magic. You can see these candles being widely used in rituals as a means of representing not only people but also things, influences, and emotions.

As the one who casts a spell, you should focus your intent on influencing your preferred outcome as indicated by the candle. If you intend to use candles to represent another person when performing sympathetic magic, make sure that you ask for permission first.

Almost every witch and magic practitioner use candles in their practice regardless of their magical tradition or belief system. Not everyone likes to use candles, though. However, as you continue practicing spellcrafting and witchcraft, you will realize their widespread

---

use eventually.

Candles represent life as well as the spirit that tends to come to life through the fire element, home symbol, and burning in the hearth. With its connection to the fire element, you can focus your intention and energy on the burning candle, making it possible for you to manifest your goal and make it happen into reality.

For you to start candle magic, continue reading this chapter so you will know the actual steps on how to perform this form of witchcraft.

Setting Goals in Candle Magic

Setting your goal is an important first step in candle magic. This means that before you light a candle or cast a candle spell, you have to be fully aware of the exact reasons for performing such a ritual. In other words, you need to have already established an intention for your ritual and spellwork.

Note that candle magic can have a wide range of purposes. For one, you can use it to protect not only yourself but also others. It also serves as an instrument for attaining your goal in life and as an aid when performing your meditation. Moreover, you can perform candle magic so you will receive enough guidance for your everyday life.

Note, though, that if you petition for something, you can't expect the candle to work on its own. The result will still depend on you, your goal or petition, and how you perform it. This makes clearly defining your goal extremely important. You need a clear definition of whether the intention for this magical work using candles is for yourself or someone else.

If you wish to cast a spell on someone, make sure that you ask for permission. If you don't, then you will be at risk of performing candle magic against their will. This may cause you to break such an important rule that witchcraft practitioners should follow.

Selecting the Right Candle

In candle magic, you can't just use any candle without determining if it is the most appropriate or suitable one for you. Pick a candle that best suits you and your needs. It should fit your spell's intention or wish. In this case, you have to learn about the symbols associated with each candle color. In the absence of a colored candle, go for a white one.

Just make sure that it also fits your goal or intention. You may use table, taper, and tealight candles when casting your spells.

Another important reminder is that the candle's size will have a major impact on how long the ritual will last. You can also find some practitioners who use engraved, pyramidal, and square-shaped candles in their spells and rituals. Note, though, that regardless of the shape and external appearance of the candle, they will still have the same level of effectiveness, provided you use the right one for the correct spell.

Also, you have to charge the candles with a certain intention. To make that happen, carve your goal or petition on the candle or anoint it to embody your exact intention.

What Does Every Candle Color Mean?

In relation to the previous section, which is all about selecting the right candle, you need to get to know the individual meanings of each candle color. That way, you will be able to select one that fits the specific intention and goal you have in mind.

Also, to create unique spells, you have to make your associations. Each candle color must connect to you personally. It should talk to you deeply, so you can make the most out of including it in your spells and rituals.

White Candle

This candle represents purity. It is vital in all fertility rituals. It is the most commonly used as white candles can improve and favor any kind of spell provided it comes with a good and positive purpose. That said, it is no longer surprising to see many practitioners referring to the white candle as the most versatile. You can use it for all types of rituals, spellcasting work, and meditation.

Black Candle

This one is a prominent symbol of protection and power. It perfectly suits protection magic, particularly spells meant to seek the help of the gods as well as your loved ones. The color black also works in fostering the evolution and development of your wisdom as well as that of the gods.

Red Candle

The color red, when applied in candle magic, strongly represents passion. With that said, it is the main color used by those who would like to perform love spells. For instance, you can use the red candle if you want to hold a ritual with the goal of finding a new lover or bringing back an ex.

It is also useful in making love potions. Basically, anything that revolves around love and romance can be associated with the red candle. You can even connect it to virility and sexuality.

Purple Candle

You can also use the color purple in candle magic. A purple candle is what you need if you intend to invoke spiritual energy. If your ritual aims to communicate with spirits, the afterlife, the deceased, or angels, then you need to light a purple candle on your altar.

Yellow Candle

In candle magic, yellow means wealth. You can relate a candle with a yellow color to any material position, such as jewels and money. You can greatly benefit from performing a spell or ritual that uses a yellow candle if you have labor relations or trade deals.

Pink Candle

A pink candle is a symbol of self-love. It is strongly connected to vanity and honor, which is also why it closely touches the world of femininity. The pink candle also aims to help in fighting violence. It is useful every time you need to create and cast a spell designed to sweeten and soften an aggressive and violent personality.

Blue Candle

If you are looking for a candle that you can use in your rituals that is a symbol of health, go for one in blue. You can significantly increase the effects of your physical healing spells and any other magical work relevant to diseases and medicine if you use the blue candle.

Green Candle

This candle is a symbol of the material world. It encompasses even the simplest forms of nature as well as the most complicated beings. It also includes all the things that live in a similar plane as other living things. You can use this green candle when performing ritual magic and spells that need a significant amount of hope.

Brown Candle

The brown candle represents the earth. It is a symbol of ancient magic that has a close relationship to the fields, fruits, and crops since people committed to agriculture are the ones who perform it. The good thing about the brown candle is that it tends to increase its strength during autumn as the first leaves fall.

Orange Candle

The orange candle is meant to represent the sun. It encompasses a lot of different fields, including calmness and peace, as well as the need to counter bad financial situations. Many of those who practice magic and witchcraft also relate the orange candle to one's ability to assimilate knowledge and concentrate.

Preparing the Altar

Once you have chosen your candle, you should start preparing the altar. Look for the most suitable area where you can practice candle magic. Note that it does not have to be anything fancy. You can just look for any room or area in your home that gives you a chance to be alone.

It should give you enough privacy and peace and should not have any form of interruption. Once you have chosen your sacred space, you can set up your altar using everything you need for your rituals/spells, including the appropriate candle.

Dressing the Candles

For your candle magic to work and produce the most favorable results, purify and consecrate the candles prior to using them in your rituals and spells. This means you should anoint them so you can charge them with your willpower and appropriate intentions. This particular step in candle magic also helps in eliminating every residual energy that comes from the source of your candle.

Note, though, that it is not a complete requirement to dress your candle before every spell. It will be a personal decision. You can decide to dress it if you wish to integrate some more power and intent into the spell.

- Pick a suitable oil – This should serve as the first step in dressing up the candle you intend to use for your spell and ritual. Choose an oil depending on the exact kind of ritual you wish to do as well as your intentions.

- Use one of your hands to hold the candle – Wet the middle and index fingers of your other hand using the oil.

- After that, rub the oil over the whole candle – Do it in such a way that you do not touch the wick. You have the option to begin from the bottom and work up or from the top, then go down.

- While rubbing the oil over the candle, visualize your intention – Imagine how it will manifest, too. Spend one to two minutes focusing on this particular step.

After that, it is safe to say that you have successfully dressed the candle.

Casting the Spell

The next parts of this chapter will tackle just a few examples of spells that use colored candles. You already know the individual meanings of the different colors of candles used in candle magic, so it is time to learn about some spells that you can cast using some of the mentioned colors.

White Candle for Spirit and House Cleansing Spell

You can cast this spell either on someone to cleanse his/her aura or your home to get rid of or banish negative energies. For you to perform this spell, you need to prepare one each of palo santo and sage stick, one white candle, and one large ashtray or a cauldron.

- Prepare your altar – You can do that by putting the candle next to the ashtray or cauldron.

- Light the palo santo stick – Once it begins burning, put it inside the ashtray or cauldron.

- Light the sage bundle next – Put it inside the ashtray or cauldron, too.

- While the smoke rises, light the candle, then chant this prayer,

"Earth Goddess and the Celestial Dome
Purify my heart
Clear my home from negativity."

- Sing or whisper the chant – You can choose how you wish to deliver the chant, but your goal should be to invite benevolent energies capable of protecting your home.

- Continue chanting as many times as possible – Light the sticks again if necessary and allow their smoke to continue filling the room.

- Meditate – Once you are ready, you can finally blow out the candle. You may also choose to let the light of the candle go naturally but never leave it unattended.

Black Candle for Protection Against a Curse Spell

The black candle is so powerful that you can use it to protect yourself, even against a curse or work of witchcraft created by your evil enemy. It is what this spell is going to focus on. It is a straightforward protection spell that can fight against a curse or any other evil work cast on you.

To make this spell work, perform it for three consecutive days using three new candles every time. Ensure that they look the same. Once you have completed the three days, throw all waste you used for this spell in the trash.

Also, if you are unsure of the name of the enemy who cast an evil work on you, you are allowed to use the word "enemy." Do the spell at night during a full moon after 8 pm.

To perform this spell, gather the following items.

- 3 black candles
- Salt
- Matches
- Knife or athame
- Disposable plate
- Pepper powder

Here is also how you can do this black candle protection spell.

- Begin this spell with one black candle - If you know the name of your enemy, write it on this candle. When writing, begin at the bottom part of the candle.

- Get the salt and plate - Form a circle using salt in the plate. With your knife or athame, cut the candle at the bottom. This should let you see a second wick.

- Sprinkle the pepper over the whole candle - Light it while saying the following,

"The light of this candle I offer to light

To undo and turn back every sorcery, witchcraft, intrigue, gossip,
envy, and evil made against (state your name) by (state the name of
your enemy) at this exact time and moment

So be it."

- Let the candle burn on the disposable plate until fully consumed – Just continue keeping an eye on it to prevent it from causing a fire.

Red Candle Love Spell

This is a love spell that uses a red candle, which can help you in making someone want you. You can cast it on someone whom you want to fall for you. Upon manifesting, expect this love spell to draw that person to your life. To perform this love spell, you need one red candle, one needle, one green thread, seven coins, and two large leaves you can draw.

- Get the candle and inscribe your full name, including your first and last name, in it - Inscribe the complete name of the one whom you want to attract.

- In one of the leaves, draw a picture of yourself – You should also use the other leaf to draw a picture of your love.

- Use the green thread and needle to sew the two leaves together –Tie them into a knot.

- Light the red candle. Chant the following:

"Earth, air, fire, and water, listen to my prayer

Bring me to (state the name of the person) who I love and desire
genuinely

I am ending this ritual without causing harm to anyone."

- Look for a crack in a tree and put the leaves in there.

- Get the seven coins and bury them around the tree, too.

Purple Candle Spell to Relieve Anxiety

As the name suggests, the goal of this spell is to banish your anxiety. It also aims to improve your confidence. The good news is that you do not need a lot of things to cast this spell. You only need one purple candle as well as your clear intentions.

- Light the purple candle.

- Take three deep cleansing breaths – Allow yourself to inhale positivity, calmness, and peace. Exhale negativity, stress, and anxiety.

- Look at the flame emitted by the candle while reciting this.

"Anxious thoughts and racing mind
I am setting an intention for all of you to stop
Doubts and feelings abound
Positive energies shut you down
Pride within while holding my head high
Anxiety can't win as I cast this spell
Clarity of mind and gratefulness, I can attain
So mote it be."

- Chant this as many times as possible – Just make sure to take three deep cleansing breaths every time you chant or recite it.

- Once you have completed the spell, you can choose to snuff out the candle or wait for it to burn down completely. Dispose of all the remains of your spell while ensuring that you do not forget to express your gratitude.

With these few examples of spells and rituals that require the use of candles, you now have some sort of idea of how you can perform candle magic and ensure that you get favorable and desirable results from it.

Chapter 8 – Seasonal Spells for Sabbats

Sabbats refer to the holidays that all witches and other practitioners of witchcraft worldwide celebrate. Those are the days that serve as the pillars of what we refer to as the circle of life, an unending cycle of nature. You can see it being represented by the sabbats surrounding the wheel of the year.

Wheel of the Year Defined

The wheel of the year that we are talking about in this chapter refers to a certain kind of calendar split into 8 parts or sections. Note that the sabbats work by dividing the entire year into 8 equal sections or parts. They are the ones that mark the start of every season and the mid-points. Each sabbat also falls into any of its two major categories.

- **Lesser Sabbats** – Also called the sun sabbats, the lesser sabbats consist of Yule, Litha, Mabon, and Ostara. These are holidays representing the start of every season. They are also more popularly known as equinoxes and solstices.

- **Greater Sabbats** – These consist of moon sabbats and earth festivals, including the Beltane, Imbolc, Samhain, and Lammas. Such holidays mark the middle point of every season. Expect each sabbat to fall on a certain day, which makes them different from the other four sabbats, which tend to shift based on the year.

The mentioned sabbats were derived from the pagan traditions in Western Europe. Basically, the sabbats are days of festivities and celebrations designed to give honor and respect to not only the Gods but also to the earth and humans.

Note, though, that contrary to the claims of modern-day Wiccans, you can't find any evidence that shows the presence of the wheel of the year in modern or present form. However, there is clear proof that the Celts, who were around thousands of years ago, had celebrations for the festivals highlighted by the wheel.

Ancient Celtic culture also indicated how time was perceived as cyclical. This means that even if seasons change, you can't find anything that's lost since everything tend to go back following a repetitive natural cycle. While the modern world often regards time as linear nowadays, many still continuously recognize life's cyclical nature.

The Eight Sabbats

As mentioned a while ago, sabbats refer to the eight festivals that neopagans and Wiccans celebrate every year. These festivals are spaced in even intervals throughout the entire annual cycle of the season of the earth (wheel of the year). Let's get to know more about these eight sabbats and how you can celebrate each one and perform seasonal spells in this chapter.

Yule (Dec. 12 to Jan. 1)

Often falling around or on the 21st of December, Yule occurs on the winter solstice. Yule holds the longest night and the shortest day every year. Note, though, that even if the long night may feel like the world is plunging into darkness, most witches still consider it a time of happiness and joy. The reason is that it serves as the starting point for the reentry of light into the world.

Once the winter solstice is over, you can expect the year's darkest part to end. This will cause the days to start becoming longer. In the all-embracing myth of the neo-Pagans, Yule is also the day of birth of the divine infant conceived during the spring. Certain beliefs state that Yule is the exact time of the year that represents the rebirth of the sun god. The rebirth is meant to bring back the light to you.

The Yule is also one of the coldest moments of the year, which prompts action to further lead into reflection. This means that Yule is a moment of thought and reflection. With that in mind, you may want to spend time reminiscing what happened last year.

You may also honor lost loved ones and family members during the Yule. This way, you can give them a place where they can participate in the festivities even if they have departed from the world of the living.

How to Celebrate Yule?

If you are just starting your journey towards understanding Yule, one thing that you can do is burn the yule log. It is a tradition that began in medieval times. You have to light up the log to encourage the return of the sun.

Look for a Yule log on your own outside. Decorate it using herbs, string, or any other item you can burn for the spell. If you can't access a pit or fireplace, then you can use inset candles. You can also perform a sunrise ritual.

- Look for a spot outdoors or inside your home where you can see the sun rising or coming up.

- Prepare a chalice containing orange juice – This item should have been blessed already. Once the sun rises, toast the return of the god.

- Recite chants, prayers, or incantations for the lord – These chants and prayers may also be to encourage hope for the coming new year. In case you need something, you may also set your intention for this ritual. You can then send out your heartfelt and genuine prayers to the universe.

- Drink from the chalice – However, leave some so you can bring it outside and then pour it into the earth. This should serve as your offering to the god.

Apart from this ritual, you can also do spellwork during this sabbat that revolves around happiness, hope, peace, love, and strengthening bonds.

Imbolc (Feb. 1 to 2)

Imbolc is a sabbat that falls on the 2nd of February. It marks the middle point of the winter. Imbolc is a word that means "in the belly."

It represents the time when the sheep usually get pregnant. Such a concept was woven into the entire sabbat as a moment of fertility, hope, and rebirth.

Celebrations during this specific time of the year often include making a sun wheel and then burning it, which is a symbol of life's continuity. This sabbat also serves as the ideal time for you to do spring cleaning. You can use this moment to get rid of clutter and begin fresh. The energy emitted by Imbolc also signifies the need to rejuvenate everything.

Apart from cleansing physical clutter, you can also use this time to clear your mind. It provides the right energy to release the old, allowing you to encourage the entry of the new. This is a good thing as it also provides room for the coming of new opportunities.

How to Celebrate Imbolc?

One tradition that will allow you to celebrate and honor this particular sabbat is to leave out some food and drink during the Imbolc eve. This could be buttered bread, seeds, grains, or milk.

Put buttered bread in one bowl, too. Leave it indoors for the traveling fairies and Lady of Greenwood. Make sure to dispose of everything the next day as they no longer have existing essence by that time.

You may also want to perform a ritual specifically designed for the returning light. What's good about this ritual is that it is simple, plus you can let the other members of your family, including children, participate.

- Start by making the participants of this ritual, including children, turn out each light in your home after dark - Light a pillar candle or votive only.

- Provide a small candle, like a chime candle or tealight, for every participant - Once it is already dark, let every participant light the candle they are holding from the larger one.

- Discuss the connection of Imbolc to fire and Brigid, a goddess - You may also talk about the fact that the candle's light symbolizes the warmth and light of the upcoming spring. Do this, especially if some of your participants include kids.

- Reflect on the meaning of darkness - You also have to reflect on the way it is a beginning and end, as well as the birth and death of a cycle. Express your gratitude or thanks to the darkness while inviting the returning light.

- End the ritual by making every participant make a wish before they blow out their own candles.

When it comes to spells, the ones that are ideal during the Imbolc sabbat are those for blessings, fertility, cleansing, wishing, protection, and luck.

Ostara (Mar. 19 to 21)

Ostara is an equinox that signifies that it is the right time to attain the perfect balance between darkness and light. The name was derived from Eostre, a goddess. This sabbat is also the perfect time for fertility. This means that it represents abundance and fertility, as proven by the sabbat's two primary symbols - the hare and the eggs.

When Ostara comes, expect day and night to be of equal length. It is a cycle that still belongs to the waxing phase. Starting from this point, the days will start becoming longer compared to nights.

Apart from being the time for new life and fertility, Ostara is also meant for harmony and balance. With that said, it is the ideal moment for you to balance yourself as well as the subtle energies that are inside of you, including your chakras, your inner feminine and masculine traits, and your dark and light aspects, among others.

When this sabbat comes, observe agricultural changes, like the sudden warming of the ground, closely. Wait for the plants to surface from the ground slowly but surely.

How to Celebrate Ostara?

One way to celebrate Ostara is to plant anything. As a spring equinox, it is the ideal moment for planting seeds in your garden. You are also allowed to perform a simple seed spell using an indoor plant.

- Pick a seed you wish to grow - During the selection, make it a point to think of an intention that you also wish to plant and cultivate into your own life.

- Plant the seed in a pot - Keep your intention in mind while doing so. If you want, you may chant or keep on repeating a mantra.

- Nurture the plant - After planting it during the Ostara, make it a point to nurture it by providing it with sufficient sunlight and water. Nurture your intention, too. You can do that by taking even just small steps as a means of reaching your goal. Expect your intention to also turn into a reality as you witness the plant growing.

You may also cast some spells that are appropriate for the Ostara. Some of the spells that are good to cast during this sabbat are those meant for fertility, finding balance, starting fresh, new beginnings, motivation and creativity, rebirth and renewal, and love and connections.

Beltane (Apr. 30 to May 1)

Taking place around the 1ˢᵗ day of May, Beltane is a sabbat that is halfway in between Litha (the summer solstice) and Ostara (the spring equinox). It is the midpoint between summer and spring. One important fact about Beltane is that it is a joyful moment representing the union and marriage of God and Goddess.

Beltane is also the period of fertility. Many believe that it is the most fertile and sexually charged moment of the year, as you can see in the blooming greenery and the beginning of the cycle of planting.

How to Celebrate Beltane?

Take a walk around nature, then collect some branches and flowers. Use them in decorating your altar. If possible, use seasonal flowers to fill it up, like birch trees and hawthorn, which are considered extremely significant during this time of the year. It is also advisable to put some green ribbons and cloth on your altar.

Moreover, you should make it a point to light green and red candles as both represent growth and love. It is also the perfect time to burn floral or earthy incense in your sacred space.

Handfasting is another beautiful ceremony that you can do when the Beltane sabbat comes. This involves two people who will have to hold hands while in a standing position. One more person uses a red ribbon to wrap the two of them.

What's good about this ceremony is that it represents how committed two people are toward each other. Even after removing the ribbon, the handfasting ceremony performed during Beltane will remind them that they still have the commitment to stay together even without tying their hands.

With the concept behind handfasting, it is no longer surprising to see it being performed by romantic couples. It is also possible to do it with friends, parents, and children, as well as any two people willing to show their love and commitment to each other.

Litha (Jun. 20 to 22)

Litha is a celebration of the year's longest day at the summer solstice. Many perceive this sabbat as full of light. It is the right time for you to go after fun and work, as you will notice the day lengthening. However, do not forget that it also serves as a mark that the days that grow longer are on their way to an end.

Litha is also a commemoration of the day when the Oak King gives back his power to Holly King, his twin brother, intending to continue nature's cycle. Bonfire, which represents how strong the sun is during this time, is a major part of this sabbat.

Note that Litha is also a moment of celebration and joy. You can look at all your achievements in the first six months of the year when you celebrate Litha. You can then revel in the warmth and light offered by the sun, as after this point, you will receive the moon's power.

How to Celebrate Litha?

Of course, the ultimate way to celebrate Litha is to host a bonfire since this sabbat revolves around the sun's fiery aspect. You can, therefore, celebrate fertility by setting up a roaring and blazing fire in your backyard. If you want, you can host this bonfire for your loved ones.

You may want to light sparklers after dark, too. Do not forget to provide offerings to your traditional gods. When setting up a bonfire, though, you need to adhere to the basic safety rules. This is to prevent hurting someone when celebrating this sabbat.

Litha is also the right moment for doing spell workings associated with health, happiness, love, relationships, luck, and protection. Another way to take advantage of Litha is to create your energy bag. You can make such a bag using the steps below.

- Collect some herbs, crystals, or any other object linked to life and vibrancy.

- Get a small drawstring bag, then fill it up with the items you collected.

- Leave out this bag under the sun – This should prompt it to collect energy that you can use in your rituals and spells later.

Note that Litha has the most energy derived from sunlight the entire year. However, you can't expect the bag you created to hold such energy indefinitely. That said, you should make it a point to recharge it by exposing it to sunlight regularly.

Lammas/Lughnasadh (Aug. 1 to 2)

Lammas is a celebration of the first harvest, which is also otherwise referred to as the grain harvest. It happens during the height of summer when you can see the fields and greens being filled with crops and flowers. It shows that the harvest is coming near.

Lammas is indeed a great moment to relax while reflecting on the coming abundance that the fall months will bring. It is also during Lammas when you should reap what you sow during the past months.

This sabbat focuses not only on the aspect of early harvest but also on celebrating Lugh, a Celtic god. It is a festival meant to recollect and celebrate everything that you have gathered and worked through the entire year. It, therefore, also shows true gratitude.

Lammas is an incredible opportunity to create a list of all the things you learned, achieved, and experienced this year. This will open up your eyes to the many things that you are thankful for.

How to Celebrate Lammas?

The best way to commemorate this special festival is to take the time to decorate your altar, home, or sacred space. Decorate it in such a way that it signifies the colors of nature as well as abundance – the ones that you are celebrating in Lammas. Among the decorations you can add to your sacred space, altar, or home that will surely add magic to the season are the following:

- In-season flowers – Some examples are sunflowers, coneflowers, snapdragons, and zinnia

- Herb clippings taken from your garden

- A bowl containing in-season fruits and vegetables

- Candles that are in the colors of red, yellow, orange, and green - If you don't have colored ones, use natural beeswax candles.

- Crystals known for supporting the season - These include pyrite, tiger's eye, citrine, carnelian, and green aventurine.

- Any grain-like sheaves of corn husks and wheat

Preparing for a Lammas feast is also a great way to celebrate this season. The feast should consist of every local ingredient you can think of. Ensure that you use grains in your feast, too. This should honor the season's abundance.

Decorate the table you will be using for the feast with fresh flowers or any of the items we mentioned a while ago for decorating your sacred space. Feast with your loved ones to rejoice in the beauty of the first harvest and the abundant nature.

Mabon (Sep. 21 to 24)

Mabon is the season that commemorates the 2nd harvest of the year. Basically, it is all about the harvest of fruits and veggies. It is ideal to hold a great feast during this specific season to demonstrate your gratitude for every blessing you received the entire year.

This is also the sabbat, which serves as the perfect moment for reflecting and looking back on the plans and hopes you had at the start of the year. That way, you will get an idea of your progress.

Moreover, Mabon is a season that holds the balance between darkness and light. This means that both day and night have equal lengths. You will enjoy a sense of harmony and balance coinciding with the sun as it moves to Libra, a sign symbolized by the scales.

How to Celebrate Mabon?

You can celebrate Mabon through meditation. For this purpose, you may want to decorate a special altar specifically made for you to meditate during this season. You can arrange apples, baby gourds, sheaves of grains, or pumpkins in this space. Include yellow, light orange, or brown candles, too.

- Begin by sitting in front of your meditation altar. Look closely at every item you arranged on the altar. Allow them to bring out safe and calm emotions.

- With your eyes closed, start noticing your breathing patterns. Breathe in for 4 counts, then out for 5 counts. Do this until you start calming down your thoughts. Do not worry if you still have other thoughts. Just continue bringing your attention to and focusing on your breath.

- Sit in that calm position for around 10 to 20 minutes. Feel the peace and safety infusing you in the form of bright and healing light. If you have a mantra, like the one below, you can say and repeat it during this time.

"Everything I need, I own
The abundance of nature and the universe will take care of me."

Expect this meditation practice performed in time for the celebration of Mabon to make you feel good and content with the abundance that nature and the universe can provide you.

Samhain (Oct. 31 to Nov. 1)

Samhain is a sabbat that falls on the 31st day of October, which is also the actual date of Halloween. It is in this sabbat wherein you will notice the veil separating the worlds to be at the thinnest. With that in mind, it is definitely the perfect time to honor everything that you have lost. This sabbat also marks the year's final harvest, which is mostly an abundant harvest of berries and nuts, as you prepare for the winter.

When holding a feast for this sabbat, setting an extra spot for your ancestors and departed loved ones is common. It is the time when you talk about them, offer them food, and honor their memory. It is because the Samhain is the time wherein you can let them join you in the festivities.

Samhain is also recognized as the new year of most witchcraft practitioners and witches. It is the renewal of the wheel of the year's cycle. That said, it is also the perfect moment for reflection. Reflect and release everything that happened throughout the year so you can finally prepare yourself for a new season.

How to Celebrate Samhain?

When it comes to celebrating Samhain, you should remember that the festival's main purpose is to remember the departed. It is also a way to acknowledge that every living thing will face death eventually.

You can enjoy a silent dinner during this time while honoring the dead by creating an altar specifically designed for them.

You may want to dedicate a special altar for them and fill it up with pictures of your departed loved ones. Add their personal items, some candles, and their favorite foods, too.

You can also offer pomegranates and apples. According to the Wiccans, pomegranates represent life, while apples represent death. Offering any of these fruits will represent the balance and harmony between the two, which is what Samhain celebrates.

Once you have already set up the altar, do the following:

- Light up a candle in memory of your departed loved one. While doing so, speak the name/s aloud. Express your gratitude and well wishes. Thank them for becoming a part of your lineage and life.

- Sit calmly and quietly. Pay close attention to the experience and your feelings.

- Take note of any message that you think you received while doing this ritual in your journal.

Guiding the spirits is also another way to celebrate Samhain. Put a white 7-day candle in your window. This should help guide the departed to the spiritual world. Light the candle, then say the following,

"Oh little flame burning so brightly

Serve as a beacon during this night

Let your light shine the path for the dead

So they will see what is ahead

Lead and guide them to Summerland

Continue shining until Pan holds their hands

Please let your light give them peace

So they can sleep and rest with ease

This ritual should guide your departed loved ones to the right path, allowing them to get into the spiritual world in peace.

Chapter 9 – Health, Wealth, and Abundance Spells

Health and wealth are probably among the results you are aiming for when casting spells. As a witchcraft practitioner, you are probably aware that you need to stay healthy to continue learning and growing wisely. If your body is unhealthy, your spiritual body and mental health will be affected, too. This may trigger problems at various levels.

Wealth and abundance are also among the common goals of spellcasters. You may also want to cast spells for wealth, especially if you are currently unhappy with your financial situation. There is nothing more frustrating than spending a lot of time and effort in your job and then noticing your whole paycheck being consumed by your bills and debts.

It is time to make some improvements in these major areas of your life. In this chapter, you will learn some of the most effective spells you can cast so you can improve your health and attract wealth and abundance.

Preparing for the Spells

Before learning some of the most practical and effective health, wealth, and abundance spells, it is important to prepare yourself for the practice first. Note that you can't expect the spells to give you the results you want if you are not fully prepared to do it. This is even more important when casting spells for wealth and abundance.

One way to prepare for the casting of the spells is to release any negativity surrounding money and health. You have to banish all negative energies that surround you and your connection with wealth and abundance.

Keep in mind that it would be much easier for wealth and abundance to come to you if you were calm, healthy, and centered, instead of being toxic, unhealthy, stressed, and imbalanced. This means that wealth and abundance also come hand in hand with health. You also have to let go of all the negativity to increase your chances of casting the spells more effectively.

If you feel like there is negative energy surrounding you as far as money and wealth are concerned, identify its source. You should then work on healing your heart so you can look at money and wealth in a much more positive light. Cast a protection spell around you so you can get rid of all negative influences. The good news is that these protection spells are not that hard to do.

Once you have done that, expect to feel happier and calmer, which is the key to attracting better health, wealth, and abundance. Once you have released yourself from all the negativity, it is safe to say that you are prepared for the spells. The next thing you should do, therefore, is to set up the scene that will support your spellcasting.

How to Set Up the Altar for your Health and Wealth Spells?

Before casting health and wealth spells, it is crucial for you to have the appropriate surroundings. In most cases, the spells are cast at an altar, which will serve as your workspace for all your spellwork.

Fortunately, it is not that difficult to create an altar. It is even possible for you to construct yours with just a small table. Just make sure that you will not be using this table for other purposes. It also helps to make the altar portable. That way, you can easily bring it outside every time you cast spells or put it away when unused.

The altar also needs to be personal. It should be reflective of your beliefs. Here are the things that you can do to set it up more effectively.

- Get a cloth that you like, then use it to cover the surface – Once covered, you can start putting and arranging items on the altar that reflect or ignite your faith.

- Put some symbols of the four elements in your altar – Line them up based on the four principal directions. For instance, in the north, put a bowl containing sand or soil to represent the earth. You may also want to put an incense stick for air in the east, a piece of charcoal or candle for fire in the south, and a bowl containing water in the west.

- Use goddess candles – Aside from goddess candles, you may also put some ideals recognized for playing a vital role in your tradition. Set up and organize your altar using the items already mentioned. You may also want to put some tools that you plan to use in your health and wealth spells on the altar.

The main goal for setting up your altar is to develop an atmosphere designed to mentally prepare you for the spell. Also, note that every item you put on the altar can help in focusing and directing your thoughts. The higher level of focus you hold as you cast your spell, the stronger it will become, further maximizing its benefits.

Practical Health Spells

Now, it's time to learn some of the spells you can cast to improve your health. The good thing about these health spells is that they can help in healing your stress and pain, as well as that of your loved ones.

Before you start with the spells, though, make sure that you completely understand how to cast them. Make sure that you are also in a good mood since it will be you who will organize the ritual and cast the spell. You need to be in the healthiest state of mind so you can attract and deliver only positive energies.

Health and Healing Spell with Bay Leaves

If you are interested in using herbs for your health spells, then among your best choices are bay leaves. The leaves hold magical power that you can use for a wide range of purposes, including healing, cleansing, and protection. The best time to perform this spell is during the new moon.

What You Need

- 3 bay leaves
- Pen or pencil
- A piece of paper

Instructions

1. Write down your intention or wish on the paper during the new moon. For instance, since you would like to improve your health and heal, you should write your name and then cross it using your petition for healing.
2. Visualize your intention or wish coming into reality.
3. Fold the piece of paper into thirds. Put the bay leaves inside. Fold it towards you, then visualize your wish coming true.
4. Form an envelope by folding the paper into thirds again.
5. Put the folded paper in a dark place that's hidden from others. If you notice your wish coming true, burn it. This should serve as your way of showing gratitude.

Health Spell During a Waning Moon

This is a health spell that you can cast for someone else. You should do it at night during a waning moon to maximize its effects.

What You Need

- 6 bay leaves
- 6 white candles
- Incense burner
- 1 patchouli incense stick

Instructions

1. Form a circle using the white candles on the ground.
2. Light the incense stick in the middle of the formed circles. Surround it with bay leaves, too.
3. Meditate. Do this until you enjoy a sense of peace and calmness. Whisper this chant but make sure that your voice is clear.

"May the health of (state the name of the person) increase and improve

By the 3 by 3 power, heal him
Rescue him from that awful disease."

4. Meditate and visualize the realization of your goal - Do this until the lighted incense burns completely.

When casting this spell, it also helps to focus your thoughts on the person who requires healing. Think about his/her good deeds and qualities, too, as you focus on the peace and silence brought on by the moment.

Spell to Maintain Good Health

If you are already in good health and you want to stay that way forever, then you can perform this spell. It is not too hard to do, and the things you need are simple. You can also use this spell anytime you feel discouraged or weak.

What You Need

- 3 candles - Use white, bright red, and light blue candles.
- 1 knife

Instructions

1. Use the knife to carve your name on each candle.
2. Once done, form a triangle on the floor using the candles with your carved name. Light the candles one by one.
3. As you light the white candle, say this loudly and clearly,

"With the light and power of this candle, I will be protected from illness."

4. For the red candle, chant this,

"This candle will lift and raise my strength."

5. When lighting the blue candle, say this loudly,

"With this candle, I will remain in good health."

6. Meditate. Once you have lighted all the candles and said all the statements, you should spend time meditating. Snuff off each candle after several minutes.

7. Set the candles aside so you can cast the same spell again the next week or month.

Spell for Depression

Depression is one of the most common psychological and mental health issues affecting a lot of people at present. If you feel like you are depressed and your case is not that severe, you can perform this spell to calm you down and reduce your level of depression.

What You Need

- 1 pine cone (if you are a man) or angelica root (if you are a woman)
- Rosemary incense branch
- Sage essential oil
- Red flannel bag
- White candle
- Paper and pen

Instructions

1. Make an amulet – For you to perform this spell, you need to make an amulet, one that can help fight depression. For women, they need to carve their initials on the angelica root. Use sage oil to dress it afterward. For men, adding several drops of sage essential oil to the cone would suffice.

2. Draw a small dog using paper and pen – While drawing the figure, say the following,

"By the power and help of this canine, I will be filled with good health."

3. Put the items you have already used in the flannel bag – After that, light the candle and incense.

4. Close the bag, then let it pass over the candle thrice – Imagine yourself feeling completely happy, smiling, and healthy. You can also do it for another person. Just imagine him/her with that positive aura, too.

5. If you are doing it for another person, deliver the red bag to him/her once the spell ends – Encourage him/her to bring this bag all the time.

After just a week, expect a major improvement in your mood and health or that of the other person.

Money, Wealth, and Abundance Spells

If your goal is to draw in energy that will give you more wealth and abundance, there are also certain spells and rituals for that. A few of the wealth and abundance spells that can give you incredible results are below.

Money Spell

This basic candle spell is one that you can do anytime. Still, it would be best to do it at a similar time every day.

What You Need

- 1 unburnt green candle, which represents wealth and money you intend to attract/acquire

- 1 unburnt white candle, which symbolizes you

- Your preferred oil

Instructions

1. Charge or anoint the candles by smearing or rubbing your chosen oil into them. While doing this step, focus on your goal or intention. Visualize the money and wealth you are about to receive.

2. Put the anointed candles on your altar. Arrange them in such a way that they are nine inches apart. The exact position of the candles is not that necessary. What is important here is that the two should be apart by 9 inches.

3. Light the candles while chanting the following words,

    "Money and wealth, come to me

    Come to me abundantly, three times three

    Enrich me financially in the best way possible

    Without harming anyone and anything along the way

    This financial abundance, I gladly accept, so mote it be

4. While chanting, move the white candle closer to green. Move it just one inch closer.

5. Blow out the flames once you are done with chanting.

6. Repeat this money spell for 9 days – moving the candle an inch closer every day. Make sure that you constantly visualize

the money and wealth you intend to receive as you take every step.

7. The spell will finally be complete once you reach the 9th day, the time when the two candles touch. During the last day of the spell, allow the candles to burn until nothing is already left.

Green Candle Money Spell

This money spell that uses a green candle is also a favorite of many. You can cast it to help you finally enjoy financial abundance.

What You Need

- 1 green candle
- 6 coins – The coins can be silver, copper, or gold.
- Cinnamon
- Green pouch or cloth
- Your preferred oil

Instructions

1. Prepare the altar where you often conduct your spells. If you want, you can meditate for a while before you finally cast the spell. Meditating for even just a couple of minutes can help energize you mentally, making you fully prepared for the spell ahead.

2. Use the oil to charge or anoint the candle. After that, put it on the altar.

3. Put the coins on the altar, too. Form a circle from the coins, making them surround the candle.

4. While placing the coins, visualize already receiving the money. Project the act of gratefulness, too.

5. Light the anointed candle, then chant the following thrice,

"Money flows, money grows;

My money shines;

I own this money now."

6. Lay out the pouch or cloth, then sprinkle cinnamon on it.

7. Wrap or put the coins into the pouch or cloth. While picking up the coins, chant the following words thrice,

"Bring money to me three times three,
Money comes from my will;
So mote it be."

8. In case you use a cloth, bring both ends together. Form a bag out of it by tying the ends. Carry it with you all the time, then visualize yourself as you receive your desired money.

Financial Aid Spell

This spell should help you during those times when you are desperately in need of financial aid.

What You Need

- 2 green candles
- 1 gold candle
- Fire-proof container
- Soft incense

Instructions

1. Light both candles. With the candles lighted up, meditate on the beauty and wonders of living without worrying about bills. Begin with the bill you intend to settle in full the most. From there, you can move down the bills on your list.

2. Create a statement that resembles a bill on a piece of paper. Write down the total bill amount and anything else that will make this piece of paper look like a real bill.

3. Focus on it for one minute or so as you imagine that specific amount of money.

4. Get a red marker or pen and use it to write "PAID IN FULL" across the bill. All letters should be capitalized.

5. Burn the bill while visualizing your will to pay the amount in full coming into reality.

Full Moon Money Spell

The full moon is so powerful that it can boost a lot of spells. Note, though, that there are specific rituals that you have to perform during a full moon to make them even more effective. Harness the lunar power even more through this money spell.

What You Need

- Water
- Cauldron
- Silver coin

Instructions

1. During the full moon, specifically at night, get your cauldron, then fill it with water. It should be half-full.
2. Put the silver coin inside the cauldron.
3. After that, position the cauldron in such a way that the light of the moon shines over the water. Chant the following thrice,

    "Enchanting and powerful Lady of the Moon
    Let your wealth flow to me quite soon
    Gold and silver, I will them to fill my hands
    Everything you can bring to me
    My purse can hold."

4. After chanting, you can pour the water into the ground. Put the silver coin in your purse or pocket so you can keep it close to you all the time.

Chapter 10 – Love Spells and Charms

Probably the most popular reason for wanting to know how to cast spells is to attract love and romance; that's what this final chapter of the book will cover. Of course, almost everyone wants to experience love. It is the most positive feeling that you can experience and share.

However, it is not also a secret that there are several times when love and relationships become tricky and challenging. This is especially true if the one you dream of does not seem to notice you. If you are particularly experiencing challenges as far as love, relationships, and romance are concerned, then you may seek the help of love spells and charms.

Attraction Spell

This love spell is meant to attract the person you love and desire. You don't have to worry when casting this spell, as you can easily do it at home. In addition, it does not aim to manipulate the mind of another person or trigger changes to all the things that revolve around you. What it does is help you leave a good impression on the one you like so he/she will notice you.

What You Need

- 2 candles
- A piece of white paper

- A pen

Instructions

1. Sit in a quiet and peaceful room. Make sure that you are calm and comfortable enough as you sit there. Focus on your intention while in that position.

2. Get rid of all the distractions on your mind. The goal here is to attain mental clarity so you can make this spell work in your favor.

3. Once your mind is free from all distractions and other unnecessary thoughts, get the paper and pen, so you can start writing down your intention.

4. Light the two candles. Allow the paper to catch the flame from the candles.

5. Look at the flame while chanting the following words as many times as possible,

"May a special someone see and notice me today

May I be blessed today without harming anyone on the way"

6. Take the ashes out so the wind can swallow them up. Never blow out the candles after doing the steps. Let them die down naturally.

It is advisable to perform this attraction spell continuously nine times. This is so you can attain your desired outcome.

Love Spell to Make an Ex Come Back

If you have an ex whom you still love, you can use this love spell. Just like the other spell we have already provided, this one is safe, meaning it will never cause harm to another person. It will not also attract bad karma.

Note, though, that instead of forcing your ex to love you again, this powerful love spell aims to remove the negative and toxic energy that may cause the gap between you and your ex. In addition, this magic can make you more attractive and appealing than before, thereby helping you draw your ex back to you.

What You Need

- 2 white pillar candles
- Sage smudge
- 1 purple candle

Instructions

1. Meditate for a few minutes first. This should help in clearing your mind from every chaos and stress that you have been experiencing every day.

2. Light one of the white candles while saying,

   "This candle is my divine self."

3. Hold the candle with both your hands.

4. Light the other candle while saying,

   "This is the divine self of (state the name of your ex-lover)."

5. Light the remaining candle, which is the purple one, while saying,

   "May we receive guidance to reach our highest good."

6. Imagine the scene wherein the two of you enjoy a harmonious and happy moment together. It should not have any requirement for attachment, though.

7. Prepare the sage smudge and burn it. Blow the burned sage over all the candles.

8. Think of the conflicts that the two of you had before, then say the following aloud while there is still smoke,

   "And there is no harm
   So mote it be."

9. Blow out all the lighted candles.

Do the spell and ritual again for seven consecutive days. Avoid showing that you desperately want your ex to go back to you, though.

Spell to Attract New Love

For this love spell and charm, you will need to use lepidolite, a lilac crystal capable of filling your heart with the expansive and nice feeling of being in love. Letting yourself become in tune with this specific frequency and feeling can help you become a magnet for such a condition.

What You Need

- Lepidolite crystal
- Full or waxing moon

Instructions

1. Cleanse the lepidolite crystal. You can do the cleansing by holding the crystal either in the light produced by the full or waxing moon or the bright sunlight.
2. Allow the crystal to bathe in the light for one to two minutes.
3. With your right hand, hold the crystal close to your heart.
4. Breathe and relax. Allow the feeling of joy brought on by meeting someone new who delights your heart and reciprocates that feeling.
5. Be grateful for the feeling and the condition of being in love. It should be as if the condition is already one hundred percent true.
6. Keep the love charm close to your heart every time you go out. Anytime soon, you will be able to meet someone new who will be your potential partner.

Love Spell to Find Your Match

Are you desperately in search of your ideal match? Do you want to finally find your "the one"? Then this love spell could be the ultimate solution.

What You Need

- New vanilla extract bottle
- Paper
- 2 rose thorns
- 3 white candles

Instructions

1. Buy a new vanilla extract bottle. Open it by removing the lid.
2. Write your name on the paper, then put the rose thorns on it.
3. Light the white candles. After that, place the lighted candles around the bottle.

4. Let your sight focus on the light of the candles. While doing that, think of your desire to find your true mate. Also, chant the following,

> *"Red like blood,*
> *Enliven my romantic relationship,*
> *Bring love and romance to me soon,*
> *Give me love as lasting as my surname,*
> *As I will it, I will find the right person."*

5. Sprinkle a few drops of vanilla extract in your room. This should help in sealing the love spells. Make sure to cap the bottle of vanilla tightly, then put it under your bed.

Love Spell to Make your Marriage Last

This love spell is meant for those who are already married but want to make their relationship as long-lasting as possible. This should also help you retain the fire and passion in your relationship.

With that, it can contribute to having a successful married life. It would be best to cast this spell when the full moon is around. Put it somewhere, either outside or inside, where you get the chance to see the moon. In case of overcast, choose another night.

What You Need

- A silver ring – It does not have to be real silver
- A small white dish
- A fresh white rose
- Some pinches of damiana, lemon verbena, and dried yarrow

Instructions

1. One day before casting this love spell, put the silver ring in a bowl containing the dried herbs. Leave it there for one day. Do the remaining parts of the spell and ritual once the full moon comes.

2. In a standing position, face the moon. Hold the silver ring up, making it possible for you to witness the moon's glowing face through the central part of the ring.

3. Say the following words aloud,

"Bring to me the bond I genuinely and greatly desire
My love for my spouse will never get tired
By the full moon's light
Bring a successful marriage to me soon."

4. Hold the rose up. That way, you can cover the face of the moon and then repeat the steps. Drop down the ring of the rose's stem. That way, there is a high chance for the ring to sit at the flower's base.

5. Set aside the flower with the ring and put them in a bowl of herbs. Say the chant one last time.

6. Make sure to leave everything securely in place until the full moon next year. Expect to witness some good results from the spell after that.

Honey Jar Love Spell

This spell requires plenty of ingredients, but it is all worth it, considering its effectiveness.

What You Need

- Honey jar
- Parchment paper
- Paints or pens to decorate the jar
- 1 pink candle
- Some plants and herbs, like red pepper, jasmine, vanilla bean, nutmeg, bay leaves, basil, cardamom, lavender, and cinnamon.

Instructions

1. Use some salt water to cleanse the honey jar. Let it dry completely.

2. Decorate the jar while using colors that represent love, like pink and red. Draw and write any word and symbol that you can easily associate with love.

3. Write this love chant on paper, too,

   With this powerful spell, I attract someone
   The person who is my faith and destiny
   With the help of this spell I am casting tonight
   Expect love to come – one that I know is right for me.

4. Put the paper with your name on it inside the jar. Add the dried flowers and herbs that you prepared earlier.

5. Use honey to fill up the jar.

6. Put the pink candle over the honey jar. Light it.

7. Look for a private spot where you can safely do your spell and ritual. Put it there.

8. In case you wish to recharge, just put one tea light on your container, then light it.

Some Tips When Casting Love Spells

To ensure that you cast love spells and gain the best results from them, allow yourself to be guided by the tips mentioned here.

Be a true believer in magic

Note that if you focus your energy on something that helps you create lasting love, it is also highly likely that your mind will be filled with more love. Believe in this type of magic – one based specifically on spirit and faith. Maintain your faith so you can finally witness your desired results.

Be specific and open-minded

One rule when it comes to casting love spells is that you should avoid using magic as a means of forcing someone to feel something that is not natural for them. Remember that love needs to be a choice all the time. You should avoid forcing it on someone.

As you recite invocations regarding open-ended loves, do not use the names. Focus on the traits and qualities that you wish your potential partner should have – among which are being loving and caring.

Understand that love magic still has limitations

One limitation can be seen in the rule stating that you should never use love spells and white magic for a negative purpose. Also, avoid using black magic in breaking a marriage or any other thing similar to that. Make sure to use the spells only for positive purposes.

Know the perfect time to cast the love spells

If you are serious about casting love spells, learn about the perfect time to do them. Love spells tend to work better if you cast them on Fridays. The reason is that Venus day falls on a Friday. It also helps to cast spells during the new moon as this phase helps in making some new opportunities real.

Conclusion

Spellcrafting and casting are definitely one of the most satisfying things that a magic and witchcraft practitioner can do. Note that even if you are still a beginner, you can still find several ways to learn and understand how you can execute this art of crafting magic. The only thing that you need would be the right reading material and guide – one that will teach you the many steps that you have to take to be great in the world of magic and witchcraft.

Note that all spells require a few different components for them to work effectively. It is also important for you to learn about all the elements and factors that can greatly affect the results of the spells you make and cast.

Hopefully, this book has enlightened you about every important detail related to spellcrafting and spellcasting. Use everything that you have learned from this book, so you can finally consider yourself an expert practitioner in the field of witchcraft and magic.

Here's another book by Mari Silva that you might like

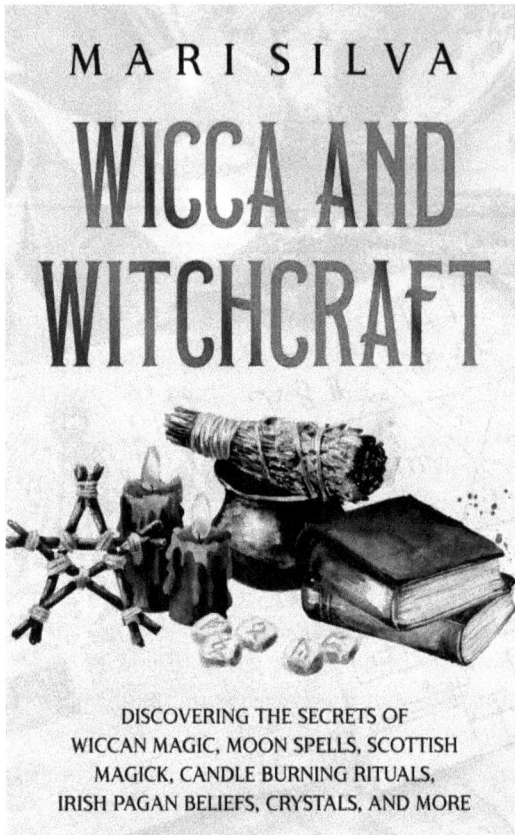

MARI SILVA

WICCA AND WITCHCRAFT

DISCOVERING THE SECRETS OF WICCAN MAGIC, MOON SPELLS, SCOTTISH MAGICK, CANDLE BURNING RITUALS, IRISH PAGAN BELIEFS, CRYSTALS, AND MORE

Your Free Gift
(only available for a limited time)

Thanks for getting this book! If you want to learn more about various spirituality topics, then join Mari Silva's community and get a free guided meditation MP3 for awakening your third eye. This guided meditation mp3 is designed to open and strengthen ones third eye so you can experience a higher state of consciousness. Simply visit the link below the image to get started.

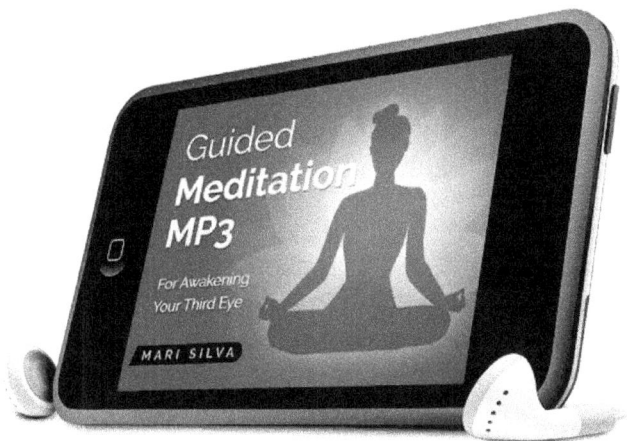

https://spiritualityspot.com/meditation

Resources

2spirts. (2022, October 8). *Protection spells*. 2spirits.com. https://www.2spirits.com/protection-spell

Basics of magic: Clearing and charging ritual tools -. (2017, June 16). Wicca Living. https://wiccaliving.com/clearing-charging-ritual-tools/

Beginner's guide to spell candle magick and colour correspondences. (n.d.). ForestofWisdom. Retrieved from https://forestofwisdom.com.au/blogs/into-the-forest/beginner-s-guide-to-spell-candle-magick-and-colour-correspondences

Beyer, C. (2011, May 8). *The five element symbols of fire, water, air, earth, spirit*. Learn Religions. https://www.learnreligions.com/elemental-symbols-4122788

Kelmenson, K. (2021, October 11). *The spiritual meaning of moon phases*. Spirituality & Health. https://www.spiritualityhealth.com/the-spiritual-meaning-of-moon-phases

Mabon house. (n.d.). Mabon House. Retrieved from https://www.mabonhouse.co/mabon

Magical properties of colors. (2017, June 23). Wicca Living. https://wiccaliving.com/magical-properties-colors/

Murphy-Hiscock, A. (2020). *Spellcrafting: Strengthen the power of your craft by creating and casting your own unique spells*. Simon & Schuster Audio.

Plants and herbs used for magic. (n.d.). Bluerelicsflowers.com. Retrieved from https://www.bluerelicsflowers.com/Plants-and-Herbs-Used-for-Magic

Samhain (samain) - the Celtic roots of Halloween. (n.d.). Newgrange.com. Retrieved from https://www.newgrange.com/samhain.htm

Shade, P. (n.d.). *The supernatural side of plants – CornellBotanicGardens.* Cornellbotanicgardens.org. Retrieved from https://cornellbotanicgardens.org/the-supernatural-side-of-plants/

Stardust, L. (2021, March 1). *How to use the moon's eight phases to live your best life.* Oprah Daily. https://www.oprahdaily.com/life/a35684513/moon-phases-manifest-meaning-astrology/

Ward, K. (2021, December 23). *Your everything-you-need-to-know intro to candle magick.* Cosmopolitan. https://www.cosmopolitan.com/lifestyle/a31133533/candle-magic-colors-meaning/

(N.d.-a). Mit.edu. Retrieved from https://web.mit.edu/pipa/www/rede.html

(N.d.-b). Theembroideredforest.com. Retrieved from https://theembroideredforest.com/blogs/wicca/how-to-cast-a-circle